Excellence in Managing: Practical Experiences from Community Development Agencies

Harry P. Hatry
Elaine Morley
George P. Barbour, Jr.
Steven M. Pajunen

The Urban Institute

in cooperation with

National Association for County Community
and Economic Development

National Association of Housing and
Redevelopment Officials

National Community Development Association

THE URBAN INSTITUTE PRESS
2100 M Street, N.W.
Washington, D.C. 20037

Library of Congress Cataloging in Publication Data

Excellence in Managing: practical experiences from community development agencies / Harry P. Hatry . . . [et al.].

Includes bibliographic references

1. Community development corporations—United States—Management—Handbooks, manuals, etc. 2. Community development—United States—Management—Handbooks, manuals, etc. I. Hatry, Harry P.

HN90.C6E93   1991   91-4265
307.1'4'068—dc20   CIP

ISBN 0-87766-521-4 (paper)
ISBN 0-87766-556-7 (cloth)

Printed in the United States of America.

Distributed by University Press of America

4720 Boston Way   3 Henrietta Street
Lanham, MD 20706   London WC2E 8LU
                         ENGLAND

The Urban Institute is a nonprofit policy research and educational organization established in Washington, D.C., in 1968. Its staff investigates the social and economic problems confronting the nation and government policies and programs designed to alleviate such problems. The Institute disseminates significant findings of its research through the publications program of its Press. The Institute has two goals for work in each of its research areas: to help shape thinking about societal problems and efforts to solve them, and to improve government decisions and performance by providing better information and analytic tools.

Through work that ranges from broad conceptual studies to administrative and technical assistance, Institute researchers contribute to the stock of knowledge available to public officials and private individuals and groups concerned with formulating and implementing more efficient and effective government policy.

Conclusions or opinions expressed in Institute publications are those of the authors and do not necessarily reflect the views of other staff members, officers or trustees of the Institute, advisory groups, or any organizations that provide financial support to the Institute.

Acknowledgments

W e are greatly indebted for the advice and counsel of members of the project Advisory Committee. They are:

Camille C. Barnett	City Manager, Austin, Texas
Linda A. Bayer	Director, Office of Development Policy, Hartford, Connecticut
R. Scott Fosler	Director of Government Studies, Committee for Economic Development, Washington, D.C.
Suzanne M. Hayes	Director, Community Development Program, Cook County, Illinois
William F. Merritt	Director of Regional Policy, Greater Baltimore Committee, Maryland
John C. Murphy	Executive Director, National Association for County Community and Economic Development, Washington, D.C.
Richard Y. Nelson	Executive Director, National Association of Housing and Redevelopment Officials, Washington, D.C.
Neal Peirce	Contributing Editor, *National Journal,* Washington, D.C.
Thomas J. Peters	President, The Tom Peters Group, Palo Alto, California
Jacqueline Rogers	Secretary, State of Maryland Department of Housing and Community Development
Carol Steinbach	Contributing Editor, *National Journal,* Washington, D.C.
Reginald N. Todd	Chief Executive Officer, National Community Development Association, Washington, D.C.
James M. Vaughn	Director, Department of Housing and Community Development, Kansas City, Missouri
Jack White	Executive Director, The Coalition For the Homeless, Washington, D.C.
Richard Wilson	Director, Office of Community Planning and Development Region V (Chicago), U.S. Department of Housing and Urban Development
Jan Shapin	Community Development Training Institute, Newport, Rhode Island

The authors received considerable help from a number of interns and volunteers. These include: Katalina Absolon and Carolyn Moehling (Michigan State University), Jennifer Marth (Duke University), Gary Goodwin (volunteer), and Mier Lakein (Yale University). Bruce Gourley of The Urban Institute assisted in the early phases of the work. Theresa Owens of The Urban Institute and Meredith Bluett-Mills of the Center for Excellence in Local Government played major roles in preparing this report for publication.

Staff at all of the Community Development Agencies visited were extraordinarily cooperative and helpful in discussing their procedures with us. The key contacts for these jurisdictions are listed in appendix A.

This report would not have been possible without the funding support and cooperation of the U.S. Department of Housing and Urban Development's Office of Community Planning and Development and regional offices. Headquarters staff from the Offices of Block Grant Assistance and Field Operations were helpful in guiding the project activities. We are particularly grateful to Charles Leof, the Contract Technical Representative, who provided invaluable suggestions throughout the work. We are also grateful for the many thoughtful suggestions provided by Christopher Wye, Director, Policy Coordination Unit of the Office of Community Planning and Development.

The work that provided the basis for this publication was supported by funding under Cooperative Agreement HA-16101 with the U.S. Department of Housing and Urban Development. The substance and findings of the work are dedicated to the public. The authors and publisher are solely responsible for the accuracy of the statements and interpretations contained in this publication. Such interpretations do not necessarily reflect the views of the government.

Contents

List of Exhibits

FOREWORD

This practical manual is a welcome addition to the considerable literature designed to help improve management and leadership practices. While many of the ideas laid out in this book are not new, past books on these important issues have focused largely on the private sector. How to apply these ideas to the public sector has been far less clear, and that is the true worth of this contribution by Harry Hatry and his coauthors.

Excellence in Managing uses actual experiences as the basis for developing applications that are particularly responsive to public sector needs. Based on the experiences of 18 Community Development Agencies across the country, the authors lay out a series of recommended "actions" for managers, organized around five key themes: remaining close to customers, encouraging employee involvement, contracting for performance, making more efficient use of resources, and long-range planning.

I am delighted to see publication of this action-oriented, practical, easy to use manual, and expect it to prove extremely useful to managers in the public sector—not only in community development agencies, but in other types of public agencies as well.

Thomas J. Peters
The Tom Peters Group

1

Introduction: What is in This Manual and Why?

The quality of a Community Development Agency's management leadership has never been more important than it is today. Local agency management and leadership are critical issues due to the decline of available federal dollars and the continuing and growing need to alleviate problems of poverty and urban blight in many communities.

Community development agencies (CDAs) in both cities and counties provide a variety of activities related to community development such as neighborhood revitalization, economic development, and improved community facilities and services.

Activities primarily focus on preventing or eliminating slums and blight and benefiting low- and moderate-income families. Activities commonly performed by CDAs include rehabilitation of housing and business properties, code enforcement, economic development assistance, shelters and other services for the homeless, job training, weatherization, and various social services such as day care, counseling services and meal services. CDAs provide such services themselves, or provide funding to other government agencies or nonprofit organizations for this purpose.

In recent decades the literature on management leadership qualities has focused mainly on the private sector. The Thomas J. Peters and Robert W. Waterman book *In Search of Excellence* and Edwards Deming's *Out of the Crisis* are examples of such 1980s management books. Public sector officials have been, and continue to be, interested in the general management literature and their application to public management. Many of these ideas appear equally applicable to public and private sector service providers, including local community development agencies.

This manual addresses those ideas that appear particularly timely and useful for managers of local community development agencies.

Purpose and Scope

This manual presents an array of "actions" for local CDAs—actions aimed at helping CDA managers throughout the country to improve management practices in their own agencies. We hope the manual will advance excellence in community development agencies.

The primary target audience is CDA managerial personnel—and future managers—at all levels, including first-line supervisors. While the latter may be less able currently to implement some of these ideas, other ideas are likely to be immediately applicable.

This manual focuses on five themes:

— Remaining Close to Customers (chapters 2-4)

— Encouraging Employee Involvement (chapter 5)

— Contracting for Performance (chapter 6)

— Working Smarter: Making More Efficient Use of Resources (chapter 7)

— Long-Range (Strategic) Planning (chapter 8)

Clearly, these themes cover only a portion of what managers do, or should do. We have not attempted to address many of the typical, but still quite important, activities of management such as obtaining financial support, working with elected officials, and selecting and promoting personnel.

The material in this manual is based primarily on experiences in 18 community development agencies throughout the U.S. We reviewed agency-written materials and interviewed over 250 management and non-management agency personnel and others, including clients and elected officials. We conducted site visits to 15 of these CDAs and drew material from three other CDAs based on written materials and telephone information.[1] A list of the agencies from which we have drawn examples appears in appendix A.

Our work focused on the Community Development Block Grant (CDBG) entitlement agencies, which are located in cities with populations of 50,000 or more and urban counties with populations of 200,000 or more. However, many of the ideas presented here are also applicable to smaller agencies.

The actions identified in these chapters were drawn both from the experiences of the CDAs whose practices we examined and from the management literature, such as that noted above. This material also provides relevant examples primarily drawn from the CDAs we visited plus the four sites that provided written and oral information.

The actions suggested in this manual are intended to be appropriate regardless of any federal or state requirements. However, we note that the federal government currently requires local agencies to provide five-year comprehensive housing strategies for housing low- and moderate-income families. The federal legislation also requires each jurisdiction to provide information on the procedures it will use to monitor compliance with the local agency's own contractual requirements. Chapters 6 and 8 provide suggestions on these two topics, which CDAs can use for their own improvement whether or not required by federal or state legislation.

Terminology

The term community development agency (CDA) is used throughout with the understanding that some entities performing CDA services are known by other names. While individual CDAs differ widely in scope of responsibility and organizational arrangements, most have at least some responsibility for such activities as housing rehabilitation, economic development, and assistance with public services—all aimed at helping low- and moderate-income persons, preventing or eliminating slums and blight, or meeting urgent community development needs. The ideas in this manual, however, can apply to managing any activities for which a CDA is responsible, even those activities not eligible for federal Community Development Block Grant funds.

Some terms have been used interchangeably. For example, CDA personnel debate whether the term "customer" or "client" is the more appropriate term. We use both, more or less interchangeably, but primarily use the term customer. CDAs have a variety of customers. While a major purpose of CDAs is to provide services to low- and moderate-income individuals or households, some programs benefit the entire community and some are aimed at businesses. Some CDA programs are directed toward encouraging the start-up or retention of minority-owned businesses, which, in turn, can directly help minorities and low- and moderate-income individuals. Some CDA programs provide assistance to small businesses in commercial districts in target areas, both to retain jobs in those areas and to complement and contribute to other redevelopment efforts in those areas.

The words "employees" and "staff" are both used to refer to CDA employees. "Director" is used to refer to the chief administrative officer of the CDA.

Suggested Use of This Manual

This manual is not intended to be read from cover to cover. We suggest that users skim through its contents, screen the list of actions at the beginning of each chapter, and examine in detail those actions that appear most applicable.

We have labeled the suggestions given throughout the manual as "actions." We do not expect every reader to agree with each action nor to find each one appropriate for use in all situations. The ideas presented are related to a number of common CDA activities such as obtaining customer input, marketing CDA programs, and monitoring contractors. The ideas are intended to suggest ways CDAs can improve their performance in these basic areas. Some of the ideas will be familiar to many readers, and some are already being applied in many CDAs.

The guidelines presented here should not be viewed as "blockbusters." It is more realistic and practical for CDAs to undertake many small but important steps, that together contribute to encouraging excellence.

Remaining Sections of the Manual

Chapters 2 through 8 discuss the major themes identified above. Each chapter presents and discusses a number of possible CDA actions. For most actions a number of sub-actions are also presented. With only a few exceptions all the actions presented have been applied by at least one CDA; some have already been applied by a number of agencies. Chapter 9, "Putting These Ideas To Work," discusses the inter-relationship among the themes in this manual and provides some suggestions for implementing these actions.

Finally, two appendices are provided. Appendix A identifies the community development agencies from which we drew examples and ideas, including contact information for readers wanting to obtain further information. Appendix B provides a list of illustrative indicators of performance for a number of typical CDA activities. These indicators may be useful to CDAs undertaking monitoring or evaluation activities, as discussed in chapters 6 and 7.

Note, chapter 1

1. Sites were nominated by HUD regional and field offices, various community development associations, and CDAs themselves. Project staff screened these nominations for relevance to the project's objectives.

2

Obtaining Input From Customers

ACTION 2.1 *Encourage Effective Customer Input into Project Selection and Planning*

2.1(a) Use public meetings to obtain customer input

2.1(b) Provide alternative means of providing input for those who cannot attend meetings

2.1(c) Encourage residents to informally survey their neighborhoods to develop ideas for projects

2.1(d) Seek input from community organizations

2.1(e) Use advisory committees to obtain citizen input

2.1(f) Seek business community participation

ACTION 2.2 *Develop Procedures to Obtain Input from Citizens and Businesses that Will Be Affected by Proposed Projects*

ACTION 2.3 *Involve Customers in Evaluating CDA Programs and Projects*

Obtaining Input From Customers

Obtaining input from customers is an important way to demonstrate concern for their interests and needs. Clearly, community development agencies (CDAs) should listen to their customers, and be responsive to their suggestions and requests. This concept has long been a guiding principle for CDAs, and has been recently stressed in the literature on excellence in management. As noted in chapter 1, CDA customers can include individuals and households, businesses, or citizens in general. Providing opportunities for input does more than let customers feel they have "participated." Doing so:

— provides better information about community needs and preferences, thus enabling CDA programs to be more responsive to those served;

— legitimizes and builds support for recommendations brought to the governing body for approval;

— helps citizens develop a sense of ownership toward their community and a better sense of how government operates, thereby enabling them to get things done;

— demonstrates that the CDA and the city (or county) is working *with* citizens, which may motivate them to undertake improvement efforts on their own;

— forges a closer relationship between customers and CDA staff.

The above does not, of course, imply that all citizen recommendations will be followed. Not all will be appropriate, and some may be impossible to implement because of financial constraints. However, citizens should feel that their views are welcome and receive a fair hearing. A number of officials told us that unless officials act on at least some of the input obtained, citizens will quickly feel the process is a sham and stop participating.

ACTION 2.1

> ## Encourage Effective Customer Input into Project Selection and Planning
>
> (Primary sources: Cleveland, Ohio; Fairfax County, Virginia; Long Beach, California; Norman, Oklahoma; Roanoke, Virginia; Rock Island, Illinois; Seattle, Washington)

Providing customers with an opportunity to have input in identifying or selecting projects, typically as part of the budget process, is one of the most common ways that CDAs practice closeness to customers. CDAs can also seek customer input when preparing long-range plans for community or neighborhood development, or when developing strategies or plans related to specific issues. Methods of doing so include meetings involving the general public or selected groups, advisory committees or task forces, and citizen surveys.

CDAs can make the opportunities more than superficial exercises, as shown in the examples below. The discussion here will primarily focus on obtaining citizen input into project selection. Input for strategic and long-range planning are discussed in detail in chapter 8.

2.1(a) *Use public meetings to obtain customer input*

Community-wide public meetings are traditionally used by CDAs to obtain citizen input. CDAs also take a neighborhood-based approach, holding meetings in different CDA target areas, neighborhoods or larger planning districts. Neighborhood-based meetings target input to specific areas from those most familiar with the area, its residents. Since it is generally more convenient for customers to attend neighborhood meetings, turnout—and input—is likely to be greater than at community-wide meetings.

The disadvantage to neighborhood meetings is that they require more resources to organize and staff. Such meetings also can, if not handled well, unduly raise expectations of residents or provide a forum for conflict.

If adequate staff resources are available, a combined approach using both city-wide and neighborhood-based meetings is preferable, since it provides more opportunities for input. What is proposed here, however, are not merely one-time hearings at which members of the public are given the opportunity to air their individual views in front of a microphone. Rather, the approach suggested here is to provide a carefully planned process that attempts to draw out a variety of viewpoints in a manner that feeds readily into the CDA's project planning efforts. The following example illustrates what can be done:

Norman ➤ To help it select and design projects each year, Norman uses neighborhood meetings in its five target areas *and* a city-wide public meeting. CDA staff conduct two meetings in each target area. At the initial meeting in July, residents develop a list of proposed projects for their neighborhood for the next fiscal year, which begins the following July. CDA staff send copies of the list to the appropriate city departments (such as streets, parks, etc.) for them to develop cost estimates for the eligible projects. Residents use the cost estimates during a second set of neighborhood meetings held in October, when residents develop a priority list of projects to submit to the policy committee. The CDA Director also provides a revenue estimate to give an idea of how much can be spent. Norman holds a city-wide "Community Dialogue" in September to obtain input on housing and community development needs from citizens outside the target areas. Staff and members of the CDA's policy committee act as facilitators for small group discussions. Each group is asked to identify potential projects for the upcoming budget. CDA staff send these lists to departments for cost estimates. Residents in target areas vote yes or no on these city-wide projects in their October meeting. The input from the neighborhood and city-wide meetings is sent to the CDA policy committee for its use in developing a CDA program to submit to the city council in the spring. Norman staff credit their extensive, broad-based citizen participation process for getting the CDA budget consistently approved without modification by the city council.

Below are some suggestions for maximizing the effectiveness of meetings held to obtain customer input:

❐ Provide ample advance publicity for meetings to encourage citizen attendance. Make special efforts to attract residents of target areas and low-income and minority populations. Exhibit 2.1 provides suggestions for publicizing meetings; exhibits 2.2 through 2.4 provide examples of meeting announcements.

Roanoke ➤ Roanoke used both newspapers and television to encourage citizen input when updating its comprehensive plan. A special newspaper insert was prepared for inclusion in the Sunday newspaper on the day a television program on the planning process was broadcast. The insert included a citizen survey, information about community development

---

EXHIBIT 2.1

Suggestions for Publicizing Meetings to Obtain Citizen Input into Project Selection and Budget Formulation

---

The following suggestions apply to both community-wide and neighborhood meetings.

1. Be sure that flyers, posters, and advertising used to publicize the meeting includes information about the purpose of the meeting, how the meeting will be conducted, the kind of input desired from citizens, and how citizens can provide that input. Make this information readily available at least a week or two before the meeting. This will give citizens the opportunity to give thought to their input and organize it ahead of time. (Exhibit 2.2 is an example of such an announcement.)

2. Design written material to be attractive, eye-catching, and easy to read. Use large type and avoid big words and jargon. Be especially clear about the location and time of the meeting, and provide information about parking and availability of child-care service and refreshments, where applicable. (Exhibits 2.3 and 2.4 present two examples.)

3. Translate notices into the language of minority populations where appropriate.

4. Seek assistance of community organizations in distributing meeting announcements. For example ask community organizations to organize volunteers to distribute flyers door-to-door in their area, to call residents during the week before the meeting, to make announcements about the meeting at their regular meetings.

5. Post announcements in conspicuous places, particularly those likely to be visited by members of target areas. Use central locations such as city hall, other government buildings, CDA offices, public libraries, and offices of organizations that provide human services. Use key gathering places in each neighborhood, such as day care centers, senior centers, offices of elected officials representing that area, offices of neighborhood organizations and neighborhood-based service centers.

6. Place ads in newspapers, including neighborhood and ethnic newspapers and newsletters of community organizations or others that are likely to reach target populations. Long Beach, California for example, publicizes CDA programs in *Penny Saver* mailers, targeted to low- and moderate-income consumers.

7. Develop and distribute publicity releases so newspapers and other media will run feature stories.

8. Use public service announcements on radio and television stations, including radio stations targeted to various ethnic groups.

9. Book CDA management personnel or other government officials on public service oriented talk shows to help promote the meeting.

10. Have CDA staff make announcements about the upcoming meeting at meetings of community organizations or other groups that staff attend.

Exhibit 2.1 (continued)

The following suggestions apply to meetings held in specific neighborhoods or target areas:

11. Be sure that written materials clearly identify the boundaries of the area included in the meeting.

12. If resources permit, mail meeting announcements to all residents of the target area, or at least all members of neighborhood organizations or other groups in that area. Otherwise, arrange for door-to-door distribution, perhaps using volunteers from community organizations. Lower Merion Township used boy scouts for this purpose.

13. Post flyers in neighborhood locations, such as neighborhood grocery stores, convenience stores, shopping centers, restaurants, recreational centers or churches, in addition to the kinds of locations noted in #5 above.

issues, and a description of the planning process and the opportunities for citizen input. The half-hour television program featured a series of interviews with city officials and citizens (as done in public affairs programs such as "Meet the Press"). Program panelists also urged citizens to complete and return the newspaper survey and to participate in city-wide and neighborhood meetings.

❐ Plan meeting locations and timing to encourage attendance. Try to include niceties that will make people more willing, or able, to attend and remain—such as refreshments or child care. Exhibit 2.5 provides detailed suggestions.

❐ Give citizens ample information about the meeting's purpose and agenda in advance of announcements, and again at the meeting.

Cleveland ➤ In Cleveland, participants are given a folder including: a letter of welcome explaining the purpose of the meeting; an agenda; information on how block grant funds have been spent; a list of eligible activities for block grant funds; demographic information on the city; and a map showing the different neighborhoods.

❐ Split up large meetings into small groups to encourage participation. Such groups might be formed around planning areas or recognized neighborhoods, as done in Cleveland. Roanoke uses random group assignment to avoid

EXHIBIT 2.2

Example of Flyer Announcing a Neighborhood Meeting

Highland Park Neighborhood Group

Invites You
to a discussion about...

+ First Avenue South Bridge: How are the traffic revisions affecting our community? What do we want to see happen?

+ Seattle's Neighborhood Program: Do we want to apply for Neighborhood Matching Funds? Do we want a voice in the City's budget?

+ Future Goals for Highland Park: What do we want to change? What do we want to preserve?

Bring Your Ideas

Tuesday, November 14, 1989
7:30-9:00 p.m.
Southwest Community Center
(downstairs meeting room)
2801 SW Thistle
(across from the High School)

Source: Reprinted from City of Seattle, *Office of Neighborhoods 1989 Yearbook.*

EXHIBIT 2.3

Example of Flyer Announcing a Neighborhood Meeting

Neighborhood   Meeting

JANUARY 19   FEBRUARY 16   MARCH 15

Help Plan Your Neighborhood's Future

In 1986, **Roanoke Vision,** the City of Roanoke's Comprehensive Plan was adopted by Council. **Roanoke Vision** provided for citizen input and direction for the City's future growth and development. The plan identified city-wide issues and objectives, determined future direction for housing, schools, utilities, economic development and transportation and developed strategies to make Roanoke's future brighter.

The **Roanoke Vision** is not complete. **Neighborhood Plans** are needed for each of the City's 45 neighborhoods to identify specific neighborhood issues and opportunities. It is time to plan for **your neighborhood!**

Be A Part Of The Vision!

Help your neighbors develop a plan that will shape the future of your neighborhood. Your input is very important.

Bring a neighbor. Meet with friends. **COME, PLAN, AND SEE THINGS HAPPEN!**

PLACE   **TIME**

CRYSTAL SPRING ELEMENTARY SCHOOL   7:00 -- 9:00 P.M.

Source: Roanoke, Virginia, Office of Community Planning, 1989.

EXHIBIT 2.4

Example of Flyer Announcing a City-Wide Meeting

Take an active role in planning your neighborhood's future!

PARTICIPATION '89

WHAT A 1/2-day conference for concerned residents who care about Cleveland

WHEN Saturday, November 12, 1988 8:30 a.m. - 1:00 p.m.

WHY To help plan the Community Development Block Grant budget for 1989-90

WHERE Cleveland Convention Center East 6th St. & Lakeside Ave. (use Taxi ramp)

Opinion, Please

How should the City of Cleveland spend $23.5 million in federal monies to improve neighborhoods through —

- housing programs
- public works improvements
- commercial revitalization
- recreation
- social services

Agenda for Participation '89

8:30 - 9:00 A.M. - registration/breakfast
Part I (Room 212):

- MAYOR GEORGE V. VOINOVICH
- COUNCIL PRESIDENT GEORGE L. FORBES
- Vincent J. Lombardi, Director Department of Community Development
- Earle B. Turner, Councilman, Ward 2, Chairman, Community Development Committee

Part II (Classrooms 201 thru 211):
Regional Planning Workshops

FREE continental breakfast . . . . *FREE parking!* (surface lot behind City Hall)

For reservations, call 664-4006

Department of Community Development

George V. Voinovich, Mayor

George L. Forbes, Council President

Vincent J. Lombardi, Director

Jack Krumhansl, Commissioner
Division of Neighborhood Revitalization

Source: Cleveland Department of Community Development, 1989.

EXHIBIT 2.5

Suggestions for Encouraging Attendance at Meetings to Obtain Citizen Input in Project Selection and Budget Formulation

---

The following suggestions apply to both community-wide and neighborhood meetings.

1. Hold meetings in a location central to target areas that is easily accessible by mass transportation or major arteries to facilitate access by the elderly and low-income population. Be sure that the site chosen is handicapped accessible. School or church buildings typically have good facilities for meetings. They usually have a number of rooms, allowing small groups to meet in separate rooms; chalkboards or wall space in rooms to hang pages from flip charts; kitchen facilities for preparation of refreshments; public address systems to remind groups of time limits and when to rejoin the main group; and parking areas.

2. Have neighborhood organizations organize carpools to bring residents to the meeting.

3. Provide refreshments (and include this fact in meeting announcements) to encourage greater participation. To encourage citizens to stay for the afternoon and to participate in small group discussions, distribute box lunches. Cleveland uses this approach, calling the small group sessions a working lunch.

4. Provide child-care service if resources permit, as both Roanoke and Norman have done for neighborhood meetings. This encourages participation by single parents, or by both parents in two-parent households. It may be possible to use staff from government recreation or youth services offices to provide this service.

5. Schedule meetings to last no more than 2 to 3 hours if they are held on weekday evenings.

The following suggestions apply primarily to meetings held in neighborhoods or target areas:

6. Hold meetings in locations easily accessible to neighborhood residents, such as neighborhood schools, libraries or churches. Norman has also held meetings in neighborhood parks, in warm weather.

7. Schedule the meeting at the convenience of residents. For example, elderly residents are often reluctant to go out at night, thus Saturday daytime meetings are likely to be preferable in areas with a large elderly population. Weekday evenings at 7:00 or 7:30 accommodate most work schedules. Check that the scheduled time does not conflict with PTA meetings or regular meetings of neighborhood organizations.

people choosing a group to stay with friends, which might lead to domination of discussion by a few people or to lack of diversity in opinions expressed. Alternatively, small groups can be organized around topics such as housing or recreation. Citizens might be invited to choose the topic of interest to them. (Exhibit 2.6 presents specific suggestions on conducting meetings.) Another way to encourage input is to organize discussion in an interesting way.

Roanoke ➤ Roanoke uses a budget simulation ("game") to encourage participation and thoughtful recommendations in its city-wide meeting. Residents are randomly assigned to groups of about 10. Each group has a facilitator and a recorder (staff members of the CDA or other city agency). The facilitator explains that the group's objective is to identify how it would spend CDBG funds. Groups first identify a list of problems, such as lack of affordable housing, then identify the three problems that should be addressed in the budget in the coming year. To do this, each participant is given three stick-on colored dots to use to "vote" for the three most serious problems. The facilitator counts the dots and ranks the problems. Participants then suggest ways to address the more highly ranked problems. To help the group, the facilitator gives examples of eligible projects in various categories (such as housing, economic development), using large colored "game cards" developed by CDA staff. Each card has an example of an eligible project with information on typical cost (e.g., $6,000 for emergency repair grants, or $30,000 to purchase and rehabilitate a vacant house), an indication of what the project would accomplish, and whether it would generate any revenue. These cards provide participants with ideas for alternative ways to deal with problems, and indicate what can be accomplished with various amounts of money. Exhibit 2.7 is an example of one of these cards. Each group then allocates $1,000,000 in "play money" among the projects, guided by the information on the game cards. Staff use the proportion of the $1,000,000 allocated to various projects as an indicator of group preferences for particular kinds of projects. This information is subsequently used in developing the CDA budget. Staff believe the "budget game" has led to more thoughtful input and has the side benefit of making citizens aware of how much can realistically be expected from CDA funds.

EXHIBIT 2.6

Suggestions for Conducting Citizen Participation Meetings

1. Assign a discussion leader or facilitator—such as a CDA or other department staff member—to each group to explain what the group will be doing, facilitate the discussion, and keep it on track. Cleveland uses the neighborhood planner assigned to each region to lead that region's group discussion. The planner introduces the session with a slide presentation on what was done with CDBG funds in that group's area in the past year. This is intended to illustrate the kinds of activities that can be supported and spark ideas for new projects to recommend. Facilitators should ensure that everyone has an opportunity to speak. For example, facilitators might ask each participant to make a recommendation about how funds should be spent, recording each response on the flipchart or chalkboard.

2. Provide training to facilitators before the meeting, particularly if the facilitators have not led such meetings before or if staff members outside the CDA are used, as is likely to be done by smaller CDAs. Use staff members who have had successful experience facilitating meetings or a consultant or university faculty member. Provide clear *written* instructions to guide facilitators, as done in Roanoke. Caution facilitators not to dominate the process or put words into citizens' mouths when "summarizing" their comments, a considerable temptation, especially to staff with strong opinions of their own.

3. Allow adequate time for discussion in both full and small group sessions, and for small groups to generate the products assigned, such as lists of recommendations. There should be enough time for all participants to express their views. This will also help avoid frustration and the appearance that the participation opportunity is for show.

4. Assign a recorder to each group, or have the facilitator designate someone to act as a recorder.

5. Put each group into a separate room, if possible. Provide each group with a flipchart or chalkboard and markers or chalk. Norman has used a student intern as a floating supplies person.

6. All recommendations given by participants should be listed on the chalkboard or flipchart, or otherwise recorded. CDA staff should forward any comments or complaints about other departments to those departments for action.

7. Provide a form so citizens can provide written input in addition to their comments at the meeting. This helps get input from those who are not comfortable speaking out at public meetings or those who have to leave early. Have a variety of collection points for these forms, including one in each meeting room and at the exit doors, and ask participants for their forms as they leave.

8. Obtain participant feedback on the format and procedures used in the public meetings. Ask participants how they found out about the meeting (to guide future publicity efforts); effectiveness of specific procedures used and how they could be improved; whether staff presentations and any materials or handouts were clear and helpful, and how they could be improved; and whether the location and time of meetings were satisfactory.

Exhibit 2.6 (continued)

9. Provide citizens who participated in the meeting with feedback afterward. For example, provide copies or summaries of the budget or plan for which their input was used. Participants should be provided with a form during the meeting so they can indicate their name and address for use in mailing them this material. In Cleveland, the CDA mails to meeting participants a tally sheet on projects to recommend for inclusion in the budget from a survey that was distributed at the meeting, and a list of the issues and suggestions raised.

2.1(b) *Provide alternative means of providing input for those who cannot attend meetings*

Include information on these alternatives in meeting invitations, newspaper announcements or articles. For example, invite citizens to write or call in their suggestions, and provide contact information.

Call-in television or radio programs are other alternative mechanisms in this regard. Local radio or television stations might be willing to donate air time for this purpose on commercial stations.

Roanoke ➤ Roanoke used television to get input for its downtown redevelopment plan using a "call-in" format. City officials and planners appeared on the program to provide information about the plan and to invite citizens to call in with their ideas. An architect drafted sketches of the suggestions as they were called in to create audience interest and encourage calls.

Surveys can be used to obtain input from citizens who would not or cannot attend public meetings. If statistical sampling is used, the findings are likely to be considerably more representative of target group views than views expressed at meetings in which a select group of persons participate. However, surveys cannot be used to probe issues deeply, require careful administration, and can become expensive, depending on their mode of administration. The use of surveys is discussed in more depth in chapters 6, 7, and 8.

2.1(c) *Encourage residents to informally survey their neighborhoods to develop ideas for projects*

CDA staff can help organize groups for this purpose or encourage existing neighborhood organizations to do so. Groups might tour their neighborhood to look for sidewalks or streets needing repair,

---

EXHIBIT 2.7

Sample of "Game Card" Used in Roanoke to Encourage Citizen Participation in Budget Meetings

FRONT OF CARD:

HOUSING

● EMERGENCY REPAIR <u>GRANTS</u>:

● $6,000 PER HOUSE

BACK OF CARD:

No financial return.

Only limited repairs can be made to house, but a large number of families can benefit. Will also benefit very low income families.

Note: This is one of a large number of similar cards given to participants. This exhibit has been reduced in size.

Source: Roanoke Office of Grants Monitoring, 1990.

poor housing conditions, and the like. Such surveys will give residents a broader perspective on neighborhood needs and encourage them to report their findings and recommendations for projects.

Norman ➤ Participants in Norman's target area meetings select five people to serve on a neighborhood planning team. These CDA-trained teams helped CDA staff gather neighborhood data related to proposed or current projects, such as measuring drainage ditches, counting trees, and conducting surveys on sidewalk and curb conditions.

2.1(d) *Seek input from community organizations*

Important ideas for projects and other program improvements can be identified at meetings of community or neighborhood organizations. Have CDA staff attend these regular meetings throughout the year, or ask these organizations to seek and relay such information to the CDA.

Fairfax County ➤ Fairfax County staff meet regularly with neighborhood organizations in target areas during the year. At an early stage of the budget process, the planner assigned to each organization meets with its members to solicit ideas for projects in their area. Staff provide information about the CDA allocation and the county's budget priorities as guidance about the type of projects likely to be funded. They also develop cost estimates for the projects the community organization wants to propose, and provide information about submission requirements and deadlines so the organization can submit proposals for funding. Staff will also help neighborhood organizations prepare proposals if requested.

Seattle ➤ Seattle's Office of Neighborhoods asks all neighborhood organizations to involve residents in their area in developing a prioritized list of projects as input for the city's budget process. Staff hold a day-long workshop for neighborhood organization leaders to explain a variety of needs assessment procedures they can use to develop and prioritize project requests for their area (such as holding neighborhood meetings, organizing a group to survey or inventory conditions, or distributing a checklist or a survey form in the neighborhood). The workshop provides detailed explanations of these procedures, and participants are given a 50-page needs assessment workbook that explains the procedures and provides sample survey forms. Staff may also assist neighborhood organizations in implementing the procedures they choose. Neighborhood organizations have about three months to involve residents and develop their budget requests. Each neighborhood organization sends its requests to its district council. The councils prepare a summary of concerns and submit that and the neighborhood budget requests to the city for distribution to the appropriate departments. After the mayor's budget request is developed, city staff send letters to neighborhood organizations and districts, informing them that their request is in the budget or has otherwise been acted on, or that they should consider alternatives such as applying for a neighborhood matching grant.

2.1(e) *Use advisory committees to obtain citizen input*

Advisory committees allow for more thoughtful, considered input than can be obtained in public meetings. A key to their success is making sure that the committee contains ample representation from the CDA's targeted customers, e.g., low- and moderate-income households and business leaders representing depressed areas of the community.

Committees' relatively small size and numerous meetings provide greater opportunities for discussion than public meetings. CDA staff can provide more information to committee members to inform their deliberations, enabling them to provide recommendations based on better information than is available to citizens at a public meeting.

The major drawback to use of committees is the need for on-going staff support, which can be burdensome to CDA staff, particularly in smaller CDAs.

Fairfax County ➤ The Fairfax County CDA's project selection committee reviews proposals submitted for funding. Its recommendations are provided to the county Board of Supervisors. The committee includes representatives from neighborhood improvement target areas and other areas with active CDBG projects; eight magisterial districts; and county-wide organizations such as the Human Rights Commission, Commission on Aging, and League of Women Voters.

Norman ➤ Norman's city-wide policy committee develops the community development program (list of projects) recommended to the city council. At its initial meeting the committee reviews the lists of projects (with the CDA's cost estimates) developed at target area and city-wide meetings. Staff from city agencies are present to provide information. At its second meeting representatives of each target area present their project recommendations. The policy committee then holds a series of meetings to select the projects to recommend for funding. The policy committee includes representatives from public and private sector organizations such as Norman's Planning Commission, Housing Authority, Senior Citizens Program, Handicapped Persons Association, Builders Association, and the Realtors Association. It also includes two representatives from each target area and five at-large members.

In addition to using advisory committees for specific projects, they can be used as on-going mechanisms for obtaining input on CDA activities.

Roanoke ➤ Roanoke has a 19-member steering committee for its neighborhood partnership program. Membership includes representation from the public sector (city agencies and elected officials), nonprofit/voluntary organizations, the business community and neighborhoods (typically leaders of neighborhood organizations). The committee provides input regarding program goals and policies, advises on staff selection, and periodically reviews program activities and accomplishments.

Long Beach ➤ Long Beach's 15-member Community Development Advisory Committee includes substantial minority and disadvantaged population representation. The committee provides advice to the CDA and city council regarding programs and occasionally suggests ways to implement or market programs.

Exhibit 2.8 provides suggestions about the advisory committee process.

2.1(f)   *Seek business community participation*

Advisory committees or task forces can also be used to obtain input from the business community, for example when the CDA is preparing economic development strategies or plans.

Rock Island ➤ Rock Island used an economic development task force that included representatives from various business associa-

EXHIBIT 2.8

Suggestions For A Citizen Advisory Committee Process

1. Include members from various sectors of the community to ensure that committee input is representative and that the committee is perceived as a representative body. Committees might include representatives selected by residents of each target area or neighborhood, or representatives of organizations or agencies reflecting various customer perspectives, (such as businesses, senior citizens, minorities, youth, and individuals with disabilities). Ask organizations represented to name an alternate to ensure representation in case of absence.

2. Set committee size so that it is not too large to allow for meaningful dialogue or to slow the process of committee work. Some CDAs have found that advisory committees of 30 or more members are too large to function effectively. However, appropriate committee size is determined by the number of meetings, the amount of discussion needed, and the number of persons needed to represent the various sectors of the community.

3. Clearly inform citizens about their responsibilities and time commitments for participating in advisory committees.

4. Be sure the advisors have a meaningful role to play, otherwise members will not be easy to attract or retain. Members should be asked to review and suggest CDA projects. Their recommendations should be given serious consideration, and members should be given feedback about the resolution of their recommendations.

5. Provide staff support for the committees:

   - Provide information to nominees about the committee's function, procedures, schedule, and responsibilities before they agree to serve. Repeat this information at an orientation meeting or at the beginning of the first committee meeting. Staff could also provide written material covering the same topics. For example, Fairfax develops a handbook for members of its advisory committee.

   - Prepare the committee's schedule. Elements to consider include: when their input to the CDA is needed; the length of time between meetings (to review any written material and to think over information presented at the last meeting); and the length and number of meetings (to allow adequate discussion and opportunities for all members to participate).

   - Make arrangements for committee meetings, send meeting announcements and agendas to members, take minutes, and distribute meeting summaries to committee members.

   - Have staff attend meetings to facilitate or help run them, provide information, and answer questions. Staff should also arrange for members of other departments or agencies to be present as resource persons when appropriate. For example, staff from Norman's CDA and other departments are present at an early advisory committee meeting to provide information and answer questions about proposed projects the committee will be reviewing. Fairfax staff attend all policy committee meetings, including the orientation.

Exhibit 2.8 (continued)

- Prepare information to guide the committee such as summaries of proposed projects and evaluations of past performance of subgrantees. At the first meeting of Fairfax's project selection committee, CDA staff members provide verbal summaries of each proposal and answer any questions. CDA staff also prepare written summaries of each proposal with staff ratings. These are given to committee members along with copies of the proposals and eligibility information. Committee members review this material between the first and second committee meetings, and vote on funding recommendations at the second meeting.

---

tions to help develop economic strategies. Members included representatives from regional and local planning associations, downtown business associations, the regional utility, the banking community, plus CDA managers. Committee size was limited to a core of about six to expedite planning. The committee undertook such tasks as: reviewing previous economic development recommendations and their successes and failures, reviewing economic development activities that various businesses and associations were currently conducting and seeking ways to coordinate these activities, providing economic and business information, identifying and analyzing potential strategies, and selecting a strategy to recommend and detailing it in an action plan.

Active participation by the business community in planning economic development strategies can provide benefits other than input. Many business groups have access to useful data, conduct economic development activities on their own, and therefore are knowledgeable about many of the issues and about the needs and views of their members. Inclusion of business representatives is likely to expedite implementation of strategies developed by the group, since their input adds legitimacy to the recommendations.

Surveys of individual businesses can be a very effective tool for developing an understanding of business community needs, problems and concerns, especially those located in, or serving, distressed areas. (Exhibit 2.9 provides suggestions for conducting business surveys.) We found few examples of systematic surveys of businesses that sought their viewpoints on needs and problems. One exception was Rock Island, Illinois:

Rock Island ➢ Since 1986, Rock Island has annually interviewed a sample of about 40 of its businesses about local business conditions and public services and ways that the CDA might assist. CDA staff mail a questionnaire in advance of the interview and call to schedule the interview with owners/

EXHIBIT 2.9

Suggestions for Conducting Business Surveys

1. Administer some of the questionnaires through in-person interviews at the business facilities. In-person interviewing has the following advantages:

    *   It is an excellent way to let businesses feel they are an important part of the community and to identify ways in which the CDA can help them;

    *   Much of the data collected can be used to help the CDA in its planning efforts;

    *   The survey can provide early warning of firms considering relocation, enabling the CDA to try to help the business and avert the relocation;

    *   the interview process provides the CDA with an opportunity to provide information on CDA programs.

2. Involve business representatives in business surveys, as done in Rock Island. Have interviews conducted by two-person teams, one a CDA staff member, the other a business volunteer. Including a business representative in the interview process—one who is not a competitor of the business being interviewed—can help achieve rapport with the respondent and subsequently lend credibility in the business community to the findings. Business volunteers might also be involved in helping develop the questionnaire or in contacting other businesses to seek their participation.

3. Systematically select the sample of businesses to be surveyed each year so they are representative of the targeted types of businesses. The same businesses should not be surveyed each year. Businesses might also be targeted by other criteria, such as geographic location.

4. A CDA can consider two alternatives to in-person interviews that can also be used as a supplement to those interviews:

    *   Send a shortened version of the questionnaire to other businesses in the community. This will provide the CDA with more comprehensive information than obtainable from the relatively small number of businesses participating in in-person interviews. The extra mailing and data processing costs will require added resources.

    *   The CDA might use only a mail survey each year. This requires a much shorter questionnaire, focusing on asking businesses to assess various aspects of the business climate and agency services. A properly undertaken mail survey can provide important benefits to the CDA and community, particularly if the findings are periodically reported back to the business community, with information on actions taken based on the surveys.

    One drawback of mail surveys is that the response rate can be quite low if special attention is not made to obtaining responses. A mail survey can, however, be sent to a much larger portion of businesses in the community. A CDA will obtain more valid information if it surveys only a sample of businesses *and* follows-up on non-respondents, than if it surveys a much larger number of businesses without following up. A 50 percent return rate should be the target for these mail surveys. State economic development agencies in Minnesota and Maryland have found that with a second mailing to non-respondents and telephone reminders, response rates of 50 to 60 percent were achieved. Without follow-up, response rates of 20 to 25 percent are more likely, figures too low to provide dependable information.

senior managers. Interviews are held at the business' office. Interviews are conducted jointly by a two-person team consisting of a CDA staff member or senior government official (the city manager has occasionally participated in these interviews), and a volunteer business official recruited by the local Chamber of Commerce. The purpose of the interview is to obtain responses to the survey questions and to discuss problems the business is having. Only some 5 percent of businesses have refused to participate. Rock Island found that many businesses were highly pleased with the opportunity to talk with city officials about their views.

This approach, while attractive, has drawbacks. First, a CDA needs to make sure interviewers are properly trained and can adequately represent the government in a meeting with business owners. Second, this approach requires much staff time for questionnaire preparation, training, scheduling of interviews, processing and tabulating responses, and preparation of findings. This means that, practically speaking, only a small portion of the businesses in the community can be interviewed each year.

A CDA can alternatively seek business responses by mail or telephone enabling it to cover more businesses. This approach will require second mailings or telephone follow-ups in order to obtain adequate response rates.

ACTION 2.2

> ## Develop Procedures to Obtain Input from Citizens and Businesses that Will Be Affected by Proposed Projects
>
> (Primary sources: Cleveland, Ohio; Fairfax County, Virginia; Seattle, Washington)

When proposed projects or activities are of particular importance to specific groups such as residents or businesses in close proximity to a project, develop ways to notify these persons of the pending actions *and* to get their input. This not only informs citizens, but provides an opportunity to identify avoidable problems.

This exchange should occur *before* the details of project implementation have been set in concrete, so the government can modify its plans when legitimate concerns from those affected are expressed. Even if the project is that of another city or county agency, the CDA should make sure that citizens in its target areas get such information and are given the opportunity to react.

To obtain input regarding public projects, the CDA can use individual contact and public meetings.

Cleveland ➤ Cleveland has developed a process for obtaining input from nearby residents and organizations prior to demolition of any property. CDA neighborhood planners develop a list of contacts for their areas. The list includes individuals and organizations such as neighborhood development corporations, political groups (ward clubs), homeowner or citizen associations, and housing redevelopment organizations, which might be interested in acquiring such property for rehabilitation. Every other week, planners receive a list of properties in their area that are scheduled for consideration by the demolition review committee the following week. Planners get in touch with the contacts on their list and call or visit the property's immediate neighbors to get their views on the proposed demolition. Input from citizens and planners about the appropriateness of demolition is submitted for consideration during the demolition review process.

A variation of this procedure is to organize a short-term committee of affected citizens to provide input.

Seattle ➤ Seattle establishes advisory committees to provide input regarding major proposed changes involving public school buildings—such as expansion or reuse for non-school purposes. Committees include residents or property owners within 300' of the school, other neighborhood residents, a resident whose home will be demolished (where applicable), a parent or PTA representative, and a representative from the school district and the CDA. The committees hold a minimum of three public meetings to hear the school district plans and receive comment from citizens. The committees submit a report with their recommendations and the public comments to the school district and the CDA.

Obtaining citizen input and keeping citizens informed can also be handled on a more informal basis. For example, have CDA staff members make presentations at regular meetings of existing neighborhood organizations when projects affecting their areas are under consideration, as done in Fairfax County.

To obtain citizen input about projects that affect their area, staff must first be aware of such projects in agencies other than the CDA. Keeping informed of proposed activities or projects (such as zoning changes, new roads, housing developments) of other government agencies (or other units in a large CDA) can be done through formal or informal mechanisms.

Fairfax County ➤ Staff liaisons to neighborhood organizations in Fairfax County ask staff in other departments—through telephone calls and memos (and as a policy statement in neighborhood plans formally adopted by the Board of Supervisors)—to put the liaison on their mailing lists for materials about their departments' activities and projects. The liaisons also review the periodic reports of the zoning and planning departments to stay informed of their activities. These processes enable staff to provide advance information to neighborhood organizations and to arrange the meetings described above while a project is still in the planning stages.

ACTION 2.3

> ## Involve Customers in Evaluating CDA Programs and Projects

CDAs should periodically seek customer input as part of their monitoring and evaluation of programs and projects. Clients of particular CDA programs should be asked to assess the services that each received or was exposed to, such as housing or business rehabilitation assistance, transportation, or employment help. Citizens of target neighborhoods can also be asked periodically to assess conditions in their neighborhoods as a way to help track progress. Procedures for and examples of involving customers in monitoring and evaluation are discussed in chapters 6 and 7.

Resources Required to Implement These Ideas

The practices described in this chapter should not generally require major resource commitments but do require staff effort. This effort will vary depending on the size of the community and the frequency and intensity of efforts to obtain input. As is always the case, development of new practices and their initial implementation are more time-consuming than application of familiar practices.

CDA staff should consider using volunteers or staff members of other agencies to augment their own staff resources. For example, smaller CDAs, such as in Roanoke, routinely call on staff in related agencies to help facilitate public meetings. CDAs can also seek volunteers from community organizations to provide assistance for public meetings and staff support for committees. Faculty members from nearby universities or colleges might be called on to provide voluntary assistance for the more technical aspects of obtaining input, such as helping to design surveys and compile survey results. Community organization members or other volunteers, such as scout troop members, could be asked to distribute flyers, make telephone calls, or otherwise help publicize participation opportunities.

More extensive efforts to encourage participation, such as Roanoke's use of television, need not be costly if local television or radio stations are willing to donate some or all of the costs. In Roanoke, the local station donated the air time and production costs, including use of its newscasters to host the program and conduct the interviews. Using public access television channels is another approach to reducing the cost of television use to promote participation or obtain input.

3

Providing Information and Technical Assistance to Customers

Providing Information and Technical Assistance to Customers

Providing information and technical assistance is one of the major ways that community development agencies (CDAs) help customers, who include low- and moderate-income residents, neighborhood and community organizations, and small businesses, particularly minority- or women-owned businesses.

This chapter focuses on providing information and technical assistance to various CDA customers. CDAs may provide:

— Information about the availability of CDA or other programs and who to contact to apply for them and how;

— Help to customers with specific problems or information related to CDA programs that deal with those problems;

— Advice about, or assistance in performing, specific functions or activities such as helping neighborhood organizations develop proposals for funding;

— Guidance in dealing with other government departments, or with others involved in projects such as contractors or developers—to mediate disputes or follow up on the status of a request or problem;

— Training workshops such as on starting a minority- or woman-owned business, or on management practices for neighborhood organizations;

— Support services for neighborhood organizations, including duplicating or editorial assistance for their flyers or newsletters.

ACTION 3.1

> ## Provide Technical Assistance
>
> (Primary sources: Albany, New York; Cleveland, Ohio; Cuyahoga County, Ohio; Roanoke, Virginia; Seattle, Washington)

Below are specific ways that CDAs can provide assistance to neighborhood organizations, individuals, households, and businesses.

Technical assistance to *neighborhood organizations* includes making suggestions about potential funding sources or helping them prepare proposals. It can also include providing advice, or identifying sources for advice, regarding projects that neighborhood organizations are implementing. Such assistance is particularly helpful to newer neighborhood organizations or those lacking resources or experienced leadership.

Technical assistance and advice can be provided to *individuals* through home visits in cases where information is best demonstrated in the home (perhaps assistance related to rehabilitation), or when customers cannot travel.

Cleveland

> ➤ One of Cleveland's weatherization programs involves distribution of a home weatherization kit to "high need" clients with utility bills $1,000 or more in arrears. Approximately 200 clients were served in a recent year. The CDA provides technical assistance in the client's home. A staff member demonstrates how to use the items in the kit and helps the client complete an energy behavior audit, which identifies behaviors that need to be changed. The staff member then helps the client develop an "action plan" that lists the behaviors the client will change. The staff member conducts a follow-up visit approximately three months later to ask whether the client is practicing the conservation measures identified, and whether the items in the kit have been used. Clients have said they were practicing conservation measures and have noted savings of $30-$100 on their energy bills.

CDAs might consider providing similar in-home assistance to participants in other programs, such as rehabilitation programs. Some rehab staff report that problems occur when homeowners do not know how to properly use or maintain items such as furnaces or water heaters in their rehabilitated homes. Brief training sessions by staff might prevent future problems and help maintain the quality of the rehab project.

Home visits can be expensive, since staff travel time is also involved. However, CDAs may be able to reduce staff costs by using volunteers in addition to, or in place of, CDA staff. Another lower-cost alternative is to contract out such assistance to staff members of neighborhood organizations participating in the program, as done in Cleveland.

CDAs can provide a variety of types of *assistance to businesses*. Assistance might be provided in conjunction with other CDA programs, such as small business incubators or loans for renovation of neighborhood businesses. Assistance can be provided to groups of businesses in conjunction with CDA efforts to revitalize business in low- or moderate-income neighborhoods.

Cleveland ➤ Cleveland uses both CDA staff and local development corporations to provide technical assistance for its storefront renovation program, which provides rebates or loans for exterior rehabilitation in neighborhood commercial areas. Two CDA design specialists help businesses in the program determine renovation needs and assist with the design and other phases. The renovation program is operated through local development corporations, which are subsidized by the CDA to: explain the program to the business owner, screen applicants and help them fill out application forms, act as the contact person for CDA staff, and assist businesses in the program review process.

Cleveland ➤ Cleveland also subsidizes local development corporations to provide technical assistance to promote neighborhood commercial areas in targeted neighborhoods. This is done, for example, by: organizing marketing and fund-raising events such as sidewalk sales and neighborhood festivals; helping attract new businesses by developing promotional materials and assisting merchants in developing loan packages; helping attract customers by developing brochures listing neighborhood restaurants and other services; helping organize and promote clean-up campaigns and crime-watch programs; helping businesses resolve problems involving city services by advising merchants about who to contact and making follow-up calls to the appropriate department to be sure the situation is resolved.

Seattle ➤ Seattle's CDA has developed investment guides for four neighborhood business districts needing development. Copies are provided to community organizations likely to have contact with businesses considering relocation, such as the local chamber of commerce, economic development board, realtors, and neighborhood- and business-oriented newspapers. The CDA also provides the guides for special promotional events and for responding to information requests. The guides are attractive publications in a glossy magazine format with photographs, charts and maps describing the community. The guides highlight features of interest to business such as the amount of retail or office space available, the number of existing businesses of various types, sales volume, parking and transportation availability, sites available for development or rehabilitation, recent development or investment in the area, and neighborhood characteristics. The guides also provide information about financial incentives available for businesses. CDA staff used advisory groups including representatives from existing businesses, residents, and area developers to develop the guides.

Albany ➤ Albany, New York's minority business loan officer provides one-on-one advice to minority clients on financial statements, how to determine how large a loan to seek, information about other sources of funding and how to apply for them, and where to obtain more extensive technical assistance if needed.

Cuyahoga County ➤ Cuyahoga County, Ohio has used mentorships to provide individualized technical assistance by involving minority owners of small businesses to advise participants in a minority business course on developing a business plan. Efforts are made to match students with mentors in the industry in which the student wants to start a business.

See exhibit 3.1 for suggestions on providing technical assistance to businesses.

ACTION 3.2

> ### Assign Liaisons to Provide Help to Neighborhoods
>
> (Primary sources: Cleveland, Ohio; Fairfax County, Virginia; Roanoke, Virginia)

One specific approach to providing help to customers is to assign staff as liaisons to individual neighborhoods. Neighborhood liaisons not only provide a way to get input from customers (see chapter 2), but can also play a major role in providing information and assistance to neighborhood organizations and their residents. Liaisons also can help market CDA programs, a topic covered in chapter 4.

EXHIBIT 3.1

Suggestions for Providing Technical Assistance to Businesses

1. Provide written technical assistance materials to businesses in easily understandable, attractive formats. Such written materials can be used to supplement assistance provided by staff and to explain the procedures of related programs.

2. Promote the program. Invite neighborhood merchants to attend presentations explaining the program. Develop brochures and posters promoting the program; place posters in the windows of participating businesses. Cleveland produced a 12-minute video that was distributed to each local development corporation to assist in explaining and marketing its storefront renovation program.

3. When using mentors to provide technical assistance, be clear and specific about requirements such as number and length of meetings, how long the mentorship will last, what kind of help is expected, and what product, if any, is expected. Provide mentors with information about the persons they will be assisting before their initial contact, both to make the mentors feel more comfortable and to help ensure that the initial meeting is "on target" in terms of assistance objectives. Such information can be conveyed through telephone contact, by mail, or in orientation meetings held for mentors. In Cuyahoga County, a recruiting letter to potential mentors outlines mentorship requirements, asking mentors to allocate a minimum of one hour a week for six weeks to work with their students on developing a business plan. A second letter to those agreeing to be mentors includes information about the business plan and a profile of the student assigned to that mentor.

4. If technical assistance is provided through subsidized third parties, provide clear descriptions to the third party of the nature of the technical assistance required. Cleveland has a three-page summary of the responsibilities of local development corporation staff in the storefront renovation program.

5. Involve local business officials in developing assistance programs. They are in the best position to know what features are likely to attract and be helpful to those needing assistance.

The liaison should keep customers informed of relevant agency activities. Liaisons can be used to provide technical assistance whether on projects funded by the CDA or on volunteer projects the neighborhood wants to implement. For example:

Roanoke ➤ In Roanoke, the staff liaison provided assistance to a neighborhood organization that wanted to hold a Halloween party for 30 disadvantaged youth. The liaison suggested potential sources for contributions, such as a neighborhood fast-food outlet to donate "children's meals" and a neighborhood supermarket to provide candy and fruit. The liaison visited these sources with the organization's president to request the donations. This was intended to demonstrate the process, so that the next time the neighborhood organization would be able to solicit such support without help. For a commercial neighborhood organization, staff provided assistance in developing an action plan to promote improvement of a commercial strip. The liaison has also helped to develop by-laws for a newly formed neighborhood organization and to generate ideas for items to include in neighborhood newsletters.

Liaisons foster a cooperative working relationship among the CDA, neighborhood organizations, and citizens, decreasing the likelihood of a hostile or antagonistic one that might exist in the absence of such communication.

A liaison is typically assigned to neighborhood organizations on a continuing basis. Continuity fosters better communication and enables the liaison to obtain a better understanding of the organization, the area, and its residents. To facilitate communication, the neighborhood organization should be asked to designate a contact person(s)—such as the president or another officer(s)—to be the main communication link with the liaison. Exhibit 3.2 provides suggestions for liaison activities.

Depending on CDA staff size and the number of neighborhoods involved, each liaison might be assigned to one or more neighborhoods. The following are examples of how this role has been structured in different communities:

Cleveland ➤ In Cleveland, a planner is assigned to each of the eight planning regions of the city to serve as a contact person for citizens, council members, neighborhood organizations, etc. Although planners do not have offices in the areas they serve, they visit their areas at least twice weekly and have daily contact with one or more local development organizations or city council representatives. Planners also attend meetings of neighborhood organizations and receive compensatory time for doing so (since these meetings are generally held in evenings or weekends).

Fairfax County ➤ In Fairfax County, liaisons are assigned to neighborhood organizations in the county's 14 target areas. Staff arrange for neighborhood organizations to incorporate CDA matters in some of the neighborhood organizations' meetings. For these meetings, the liaison prepares and distributes meeting announcements to residents, and takes and distributes minutes. Liaisons generally attend two to five meetings per year in each target area, depending on whether any projects are taking place in that area. They serve as contacts for neighborhood organizations, answer questions, and resolve problems. The liaisons also provide information and referral on request, as well as technical assistance.

EXHIBIT 3.2

Suggestions for Neighborhood Liaison Activities

1. If liaisons are assigned to neighborhoods rather than neighborhood organizations, they should attend regular meetings of various organizations in that neighborhood. If there are a large number of organizations, the liaison might attend the meetings of some groups one month, and of others the next. An arrangement may be needed to provide liaisons with compensatory time for meetings they attend, since most neighborhood organization meetings are likely to be scheduled during the evening.

2. Make liaisons available on a regular basis, perhaps one afternoon or morning every week or two at specific times and places—for example, at the office of a neighborhood organization or other recognized "meeting place" such as a community center—so residents know where and when liaisons can be reached.

3. Have liaisons serve as a contact and referral point in the CDA for neighborhood organizations to call with questions or concerns regarding community development matters. Liaisons should respond promptly, even if questions are not directly related to CDA matters. This demonstrates to neighborhood organizations that the liaison is on their side.

4. Maintain frequent contact even when there is no particular issue or event to discuss. For example, in Roanoke, the liaison calls each neighborhood organization leader at least once a month to keep in touch. Note that this is *in addition to* calls that neighborhood organization leaders might make to the liaison, or calls the liaison might make to leaders regarding specific issues. In addition to such telephone contact, liaisons might drop in at the office neighborhood organization when in the area.

5. Prepare and distribute a newsletter to keep neighborhood organizations and citizens informed of community development activities. Ask each neighborhood organization to submit relevant items for each issue. Send the newsletter to each neighborhood organization and place copies in key neighborhood locations such as convenience stores, churches, and libraries. If a CDA newsletter is produced by another unit in the CDA, have a section in it for liaison use to report on neighborhood organization activities, make announcements, and so on.

6. Provide information about upcoming events of interest to neighborhood organizations. In Roanoke, the liaison prepares a monthly calendar listing of all events related to the partnership program, including meetings of neighborhood organizations, neighborhood festivals or special events, and workshops or meetings sponsored by the partnership office. The calendar is sent to the president of each neighborhood organization in the partnership about a week before the beginning of the month so they can notify their members. It is also sent to the major newspaper, which publishes each week's portion in its weekly "Neighborhoods" section.

7. Encourage neighborhood organizations to keep their liaisons—and the CDA—informed. In Roanoke, all neighborhood organizations that produce newsletters are asked to send copies to the liaison. This helps keep staff informed about what is happening in the neighborhood and what issues are of concern to residents.

Roanoke ➤ In Roanoke, one neighborhood planner serves as liaison to 21 neighborhood organizations in the neighborhood partnership program. The liaison performs most of the activities in exhibit 3.2.

Since the intent of the neighborhood liaison role is to create closeness to customers, it is important that the liaisons do not become another bureaucratic mechanism facing neighborhood organizations. Liaisons should be supportive and act informally; they should be individuals who enjoy, and are good at, meeting and talking with people. The CDA should be sure that the liaisons work well with the neighborhoods, lest the effort become counter-productive.

Liaisons should be honest about their limits and not suggest they will take care of problems not in their control. They should make it clear that the intent of technical assistance is to help neighborhood organizations learn to do things independently, not to become dependent on them. Finally, liaisons should provide advice and guidance without dictating to neighborhood organizations.

The liaison function can require a substantial commitment of staff resources. The CDA can design its liaison function to accommodate its resource constraints, making the liaison concept highly transferable. For instance, some or all staff members in a particular division or job classification might have liaison responsibilities as part of their job, as in Fairfax County and Cleveland. Alternatively, being the liaison might be the primary responsibility of one or two staff members, as in Roanoke.

CDAs can control resource use by assigning liaisons only to selected neighborhood organizations—for example, those in target areas, or those participating in particular programs.

ACTION 3.3

Provide Training Workshops

(Primary sources: Cleveland, Ohio; Cuyahoga County, Ohio; Roanoke, Virginia; Seattle, Washington)

Training workshops are efficient when a group of people can benefit from the same kind of assistance. Also, workshops enable participants to get to know each other and to learn about other parts of the community.

Workshops can be held *for neighborhood organizations* to provide management-related training in areas such as proposal writing, fundraising, grant administration, or leadership skills. Workshops might be taught by CDA staff, particularly if the topic is closely related to CDA responsibilities (such as writing proposals for CDA grants), or by others, particularly if special skills are required.

Roanoke ➤ Roanoke contracts with a consultant to develop and administer four workshops each year for neighborhood organization leaders. Recent topics included: grant-writing, media relations, and sponsoring special events. Roanoke's grants monitor provides an annual grant administration workshop for neighborhood organizations receiving mini-grants or incentive grants. This focuses on rules and procedures, particularly regarding bookkeeping and reporting requirements.

Seattle ➤ Seattle provides training workshops for neighborhood organization leaders in fundraising and leadership skills, such as facilitating meetings, resolving conflicts and creating change, as well as in needs assessment methods. Training has been provided by consultants, staff members, university faculty, and leaders of neighborhood organizations.

Cleveland ➤ Cleveland staff provide weatherization and energy savings workshops for citizens at neighborhood organization meetings and in conjunction with city-sponsored events such as the annual home and flower show or "senior day."

Workshops can also be held for *minority-owned and other small businesses,* as structured "classes" or as presentations, seminars, or discussion groups. The following topics have been found to be useful areas to cover in such workshops: how to establish a business and develop a business plan; paperwork requirements associated with government programs; estimating and bidding; marketing; bookkeeping and financial statements; obtaining loans and other financial assistance; taxes and tax preparation; government regulations; how to obtain a good lawyer or accountant; budgeting; financial and cash flow management; insurance; employee benefits; and computer training.

Cuyahoga County ➤ Cuyahoga County's Minority Business Development Program offers a sequence of two formally structured courses on starting a business. The first course consists of two day-long sessions held on Saturdays on topics related to starting a business. The second course, developing a business plan, is taught one evening per week at the community college for a 14-week period. Continuing education credits are provided for this course. Both courses are taught by minority business people and include guest lectures by minority business owners and professionals such as accountants, attorneys and bankers. The second course includes a mentorship arrangement between students and owners of small minority businesses.

Albany ➤ In Albany, the CDA refers individuals seeking training or technical assistance to a nonprofit organization developed to provide training for minorities wishing to own businesses. This organization, affiliated with the state university and the Chamber of Commerce, provides periodic half-day or day-long workshops on starting a business and holds series of "round-table" discussions with minority business owners on topics related to starting a business. The discussions are structured in a small-group (8-10) format to promote interaction.

Exhibit 3.3 provides suggestions for workshops, including a separate section about workshops for minority or small businesses.

Resources Required. Because of the special skills needed for conducting effective workshops, they can be costly. The CDA might make such assistance partly self-supporting by charging workshop or class fees. In Cuyahoga County, fees for the minority-business training course help support the program and provide an incentive for participants to complete the course. The CDA might also be able to use volunteers from the business community to cut down on costs, or get a local college or business organization to subsidize the effort.

ACTION 3.4

Provide Information Materials to Customers
(Primary sources: Cleveland, Ohio; Cuyahoga County, Ohio; Roanoke, Virginia)

In addition to providing workbooks to accompany technical assistance or training workshops, CDAs should also develop self-guided training or information materials for clients. The material is likely to be more effective if staff are available to answer questions and provide assistance to recipients. The availability of such assistance can be made clear in letters accompanying the material or on the cover page or introduction to the written materials.

Roanoke ➤ Roanoke had faculty members from a nearby university develop a guidebook on how to incorporate neighborhood organizations as nonprofit organizations.

Cuyahoga County ➤ Cuyahoga County developed a fair housing reference manual for its participating municipalities. The manual describes fair housing organizations and the services they provide, as well as various federal, state, and local fair housing legislation. Updates to the manual are provided to the municipalities as needed.

EXHIBIT 3.3

Suggestions for Training Workshops

1. Seek input from the target audience to help select topics that will serve their needs and interests. This might be done through a questionnaire distributed to all neighborhood organization leaders. CDAs can also obtain such information from participants in previous workshops. Survey those seeking assistance on their training needs. For example, in Albany's minority business assistance program, client intake forms ask what kind of training workshops clients are interested in.

2. Arrange the timing and location of workshops for the convenience of participants. Check that dates and times do not conflict with other neighborhood organization meetings. Seek input from the target audience about "best times" and locations, perhaps in the questionnaire used to obtain input on topics. For example, in Roanoke, workshops start at 5:45 or 6:00 p.m. so participants can leave by about 8:00.

3. Limit workshop size to facilitate personal attention and interaction between participants and trainer. This also makes it easier to arrange for "hands on" application of the information provided. Workshops with more than 20-25 people are likely to become cumbersome, especially if they do not include small group breakout sessions.

4. Publicize workshops well in advance through mailings. Place announcements in neighborhood newspapers and other appropriate places that will reach the target audience 2 to 3 weeks before the workshop. Allow 4 to 6 weeks of lead time when sending announcements to neighborhood organization leaders to distribute or announce at their meetings.

5. Make workshop publicity materials informative and attractive. Be sure that announcements provide information on the topic, not just the title of the workshop, as well as on timing and location. Include logistical information about parking, refreshments, etc., and a number to call for more information. Design announcements to sell the workshop—include favorable comments from prior participants or indications of why the workshop is useful. Exhibit 3.4 is an example of such an announcement.

6. Provide handouts to workshop participants to enhance learning. Media workshop handouts in Roanoke include a list of contact names and sample press releases. Seattle provides a Needs Assessment Workbook as part of its workshop on this topic.

7. Provide evaluation forms after each workshop to obtain suggestions for improvements and recommendations for future workshop topics. Include questions about participants' satisfaction with topic, content, presentation of material, the instructor(s), handouts or other materials, length, timing and location of workshop, and any other topic on which the CDA wants feedback. Use ratings such as poor, fair, good, and, excellent. Include an open-ended question asking for recommendations for improvement. Ask how participants heard about the workshop, to help guide future publicity efforts. Include a question on future workshop topics, listing topics staff think might be of interest and including space for participants to recommend others.

8. Provide recognition for volunteers, such as mentors or those who provide guest lectures or other kinds of assistance. This could be in the form of certificates or plaques, presented at a recognition event such as a luncheon or reception sponsored by the CDA. If there is a graduation ceremony for participants, this can also be used as an opportunity to recognize volunteers. At a minimum, send thank you letters to volunteers and recognize their contributions in CDA newsletters.

Exhibit 3.3 (continued)

Suggestions for Training Workshops for Small and Minority Businesses

1. Use business people in the relevant field to provide training and technical assistance. This provides participants with opportunities to make contacts. Where possible, minority trainers should be used. Groups that might provide or help locate and recruit individuals with such expertise include:

    *   The Chamber of Commerce, which may have sub-chambers for minority- and women-owned business and small business, and other business or professional associations;

    *   Universities, community colleges, trade or vocational education schools, which might provide faculty members or graduate students to provide training and technical assistance;

    *   Retired executives volunteer programs; and

    *   Government organizations, such as the Small Business Association or local economic development organizations.

2. Obtain input from minority business representatives to guide training efforts. Consider creating an advisory board or committee composed of members of the local minority business community and others who have insight into training needs, such as educators and representatives of financial institutions or economic development organizations. Seek their advice regarding content of training or technical assistance; individuals to serve as instructors, guest lecturers, or mentors; and how to best publicize training and assistance opportunities. Cuyahoga County used an advisory committee to develop its training program. Members included minority business people, bankers, representatives of universities and community colleges and of economic development agencies.

3. Provide recognition for students who have completed formal minority business enterprise training programs. Cleveland holds a graduation ceremony for students completing its construction management training seminar. This event includes a keynote speaker, such as the mayor, and remarks by individuals such as the city's EEO officer. A reception with refreshments is also provided.

4. Use the targeted marketing approach suggested in chapter 4 to market training programs to minority businesses. Send announcements to participants in prior training efforts so they can notify co-workers. Focus promotional efforts on business or training-related organizations, such as minority sub-chambers of the Chamber of Commerce, federal state and local agencies that are likely to have minority business programs, and colleges, community colleges or trade schools, particularly those with high minority enrollments. Advertise on business-oriented radio or television programs. Seek visibility through staff participation in minority business workshops or seminars. The director of Cuyahoga County's minority business development program frequently makes presentations on its training opportunities to business- and minority-oriented groups.

EXHIBIT 3.4

Example of Workshop Announcement

F
R
E
E

Volunteer leaders are strongly encouraged to register for the entire series at a single location.

Where: University Christian Church
Lower Lounge
4731 15th NE

Meeting Facilitation: Thurs, Oct. 26, 1989
7:00 - 9:45 pm

Creating Change: Sat, Oct. 28, 1989
10:00 am - 3:00 pm

Where: Catholic Community Services
"Great Room"
100 23rd Ave S (23rd and Yesler)

Meeting Facilitation: Thur, Nov. 9, 1989
7:00 - 9:45 pm

Creating Change: Sat, Nov. 11, 1989
10:00 am - 3:00 pm

W
O
R
K
S
H
O
P
S

Course A: The Art of Meeting Facilitation

The new leader is a facilitator. Community, consensus and teamwork are all built from groups and groups are dependent on meetings. This course will introduce you to the skills, procedures and groundrules for holding productive group discussion and achieving consensus through the meeting process. Some of the topics to be covered are:

○ Agendas that achieve your purpose

○ Guidelines for the facilitator

○ Techniques for group discussion: identifying issues, evaluating and prioritizing ideas, reaching consensus

○ Techniques for resolving meeting conflicts and dilemmas

Course B: Leadership in Creating Change

Being an effective advocate for your own organization's goals requires the ability to resolve conflicts, develop cooperation, communicate with others and negotiate effectively for the changes you want. In this course you will increase your skills in:

○ Building rapport and gaining participation

○ Listening and communicating under pressure

○ Dealing with differences and resolving conflicts

○ Using principled negotiation skills

F
R
E
E

Graduates found the series extremely helpful and have said so ! ! !

66 *Very good training. I will use this information at my next meeting. . . tomorrow!* 99

66*Practical ideas we can use right away. The facilitator (instructor) was great.* 99

66*Good techniques to try, good written materials, thanks!* 99

66*She (instructor) showed how to best lead a meeting.* 99

66*This was a great experience. Thanks.* 99

Call 684-0464 to register or for more information.
Space Limited. Register Early.

Source: Reprinted from City of Seattle, *Office of Neighborhoods 1989 Yearbook.*

Because citizens may call elected representatives or other agencies rather than the CDA with questions about community development matters, CDA staff should provide basic information on frequently asked questions to elected officials and staff of other agencies. This information should be updated periodically, and appropriate CDA telephone numbers should be prominently featured.

Cleveland   ➤ Cleveland developed a brochure called "A Pocket Guide to Demolition for Councilmen" to help elected officials answer constituents' questions about demolition.

When preparing written material for citizens, easy-to-read formats should be used with illustrations or diagrams to reinforce key point. This is particularly important for clients with poor reading skills. Large type is essential for materials intended for the elderly. CDAs can learn from Madison Avenue advertising techniques!

Cleveland   ➤ Cleveland includes an attractive calendar in its weatherization kit that highlights energy saving tips, accompanied by illustrations of key concepts (see exhibit 3.5). Calendar pages provide room for homeowners to write down their energy saving plans. The calendar is designed for two years so it will be used longer. The kit also includes a coloring book for the homeowner's children that reinforces the information provided to parents, and includes cost-saving behaviors children can adopt, such as turning off lights and appliances and closing the refrigerator door (see exhibit 3.6). The coloring book educates both children and parents, and keeps the children busy when the staff member conducts the energy audit with the parent.

Similar formats might be used to present tips about home maintenance (for rehabilitation clients) or community improvement such as anti-littering or clean-up efforts.

Developing and providing informational materials can be costly, though it may be possible to save on development costs by adapting materials developed elsewhere.

ACTION 3.5

Make Sure Customers Have Adequate Information on Their Rights and Obligations
(Primary sources: Lower Merion Township, Pennsylvania; Norman, Oklahoma; Rock Island, Illinois)

Clients may not always understand their rights in connection with CDA projects—for example, that rehabilitation work is

EXHIBIT 3.5

Example of Informational Material in Useful Format

WILBER FORGETS TO LOWER
THE THERMOSTAT ON HIS
WATER HEATER.

HOT WATER HEATERS

You can save energy if you don't overheat your water, because the hotter the water, the faster the heat is lost. Most feel that a hot water temperature of 110 or 120 degrees is sufficient for their cleaning needs. Turn down the temperature setting by adjusting the dial that is usually located near the pilot light; change it from a "hot" or "high" temperature setting to a "warm" or "low" setting. On electric hot water heaters, there may be two separate heating elements, therefore turn down the thermostat on both. Cooler temperature settings save you money by reducing heat lost through the water heater tank and pipes. Remember that your hot water heater is another large energy user in your home.

Washing and Shaving

Don't waste hot water needlessly. Plug the drain when you wash and shave. Also, turn the water off and on instead of letting it run constantly.

Washing Dishes and Clothes

When washing dishes by hand, rinse the dishes at the same time. When possible, do only full loads while washing clothes. Use cold water with a cold water detergent.

MY ENERGY SAVING PLANS:

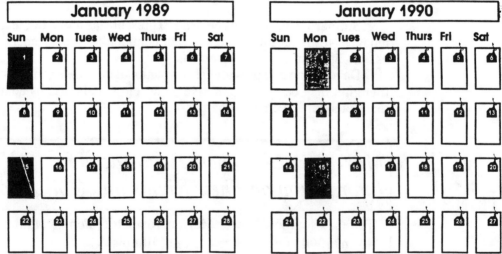

Source: State of Ohio Office of Weatherization, Energy Conservation 1989-1990 Calendar.

EXHIBIT 3.6

Example of Informational Material in Attractive Format
(Coloring book with energy saving tips)

Lights and TV sets like to be turned off when they're not in use.

Source: Cleveland, Ohio Department of Community Development, "How We Save Energy" coloring book, 1990.

under a one-year warranty from the contractors. While clients may be initially aware of the warranty, they may not realize or may forget how long it lasts or what it covers. A number of actions can alert clients to their rights, particularly the elderly, whose memories may not be good, and those whose ability to read detailed warranty statements may be limited.

❏ Explain what will happen during projects so customers know what to expect, especially from the contractor. Explain customers' obligations, such as choices they must make and adhere to. Make clear what the service covers and what it does not.

Norman ➤ Norman's rehab staff make customers aware of the normal inconveniences associated with rehab work—for example, that their kitchens or bathrooms will be torn up and unusable for a period of time—to avert dissatisfaction or complaints.

❏ Clearly explain the warranty provisions at the final check-off of the property and urge customers to contact staff with any problem, as done in Norman. In addition, rehab staff should explain that a warranty letter will be sent to customers from the contractor. This letter should clearly explain the contractor's obligations under the warranty.

❏ At the time of sign-off of the work, provide clients with a highly noticeable warranty announcement that simply, and in big bright letters, summarizes their rights and the date of expiration of the warranty. While it still remains the homeowner's responsibility to complain when necessary, the physical appearance of the warranty makes it more likely that clients will be aware of their rights and of the warranty expiration date.

❏ Send a reminder letter to clients a month or two before the warranty expires. Notify them that the warranty will soon expire and that they should notify the agency if there are any problems relating to the work done by the contractors. Most agency personnel with whom we spoke, particularly rehabilitation inspectors, were concerned that this would open up a Pandora's box of complaints from clients. They were afraid that clients would make numerous complaints, most of which would not be covered by the warranty. However, on balance, this concern is secondary to making sure that clients and the CDA get what they contracted for.

❐ Contact each client by phone or in person a few weeks before the warranty expires to remind them to check the work covered by the warranty, as is done in Rock Island.

ACTION 3.6

> ## *Help Customers in Their Dealings with Government Agencies*
>
> (Primary sources: Cleveland, Ohio; Long Beach, California; Roanoke, Virginia)

Many people feel intimidated by the idea of dealing with government agencies, including the CDA itself. Citizens are often confused by the number of agencies, and are unsure of where to seek assistance. In cases where citizens are trying to resolve problems—perhaps related to the actions (or inactions) of a particular agency—they may feel they are unlikely to receive a fair hearing, or that they may not be understood. This is particularly likely if English is not their primary language or if they are not well-educated or experienced in dealing with government agencies. Citizens can quickly become dissatisfied with long delays in resolving problems, feeling that the bureaucracy has stuck it to them again. CDAs can improve their services by helping customers deal with government agencies, both formally and informally.

3.6(a) *Informally facilitate customers' dealings with other government agencies (or other units of the CDA)*

Staff can provide both moral support and advice to customers, can help explain things that may be unclear and help mediate discussions.

Roanoke ➤ In Roanoke, neighborhood liaisons sit in on meetings neighborhood organizations have with other city departments on request (for example, when the neighborhood organization is having a problem with, or making a request of, another department). Staff believe this prevents antagonism between the city and its neighborhoods and helps neighborhood organizations work within the system.

Long Beach ➤ Long Beach includes representatives from other city departments at community meetings it sponsors. Depending on the topic, the CDA provides representatives from such agencies as Parks and Recreation, Zoning, Police, etc. Long Beach has found that regardless of the announced purpose of the meeting, inevitably citizens will raise other concerns that can best be handled by other city agencies. By inviting other departments, the CDA assures a quick response to citizen concerns.

3.6(b)   *Provide a formal mediation or "ombudsman" service*

This service serves as a sounding board and as representation for clients when there is a problem or complaint. Some local governments already have government-wide ombudsman programs. A CDA itself might want to establish such a system on either a formal or informal basis.

Cleveland   ➤ Cleveland established an "ombudsman" office in its Division of Buildings and Housing to help resolve problems and complaints related to various kinds of building permits. Most complaints involve unreasonable delays. Although the primary users of this service are contractors and developers, more citizens and neighborhood organizations are beginning to use it as well. The ombudsman office is staffed by one person, with clerical support provided by other parts of the division. When a complaint comes in, the ombudsman gathers information from the customer, then talks to staff responsible for processing the disputed permit. In cases where the customer did not follow procedures or submit enough information, the ombudsman explains the system to the customer and often acts as an intermediary to obtain and transmit the information necessary to keep the permit process moving.

An ombudsman (or another CDA staff member) could also take a proactive approach to problems. For example, staff could be assigned to streamline the system or monitor progress of permits or other documents to reduce complaints.

Cleveland   ➤ Cleveland's ombudsman uses a manual database to track the progress of all permits from application to final disposition. If a permit is taking too long, the ombudsman follows up with department staff to determine whether there is a problem and to request they speed up the process. The ombudsman also makes recommendations to manage-

The ombudsman office also issues periodic reports on the number and types of complaints received, to help identify areas where improvements are needed.

3.6(c) *Provide mechanisms to facilitate citizens' requests and to keep them informed of the status of requests or projects*

Issue periodic mailings to citizens who are on waiting lists of any kind to inform them of the status of their request and to provide an estimated date for when they are likely to be served.

Roanoke ➤ Roanoke administers an "Eyesore Alert" program. Each participating neighborhood organization identifies two priority eyesores each month, typically junk cars and weed-filled or littered lots. The neighborhood organization uses a form to notify CDA staff, who alert the appropriate city department and keep track of progress about the complaint. Staff notify the neighborhood organization about the status of the complaint within 30 days. The program guarantees that action on the eyesore will be taken by the appropriate department within 30 days (although the eyesore is not always removed in 30 days).

ACTION 3.7

> ## *Provide Capacity-Building Assistance for Neighborhood Organizations and Small or Minority Businesses*
>
> (Primary sources: Albany, New York; Fairfax County, Virginia; Knoxville, Tennessee; Roanoke, Virginia; Rock Island, Illinois; Seattle, Washington)

CDAs can promote the survival and flourishing of neighborhood organizations and small or minority businesses through capacity-building support. This support goes over and beyond the technical assistance described earlier in this chapter. Capacity-building support may involve directly or indirectly subsidizing some activities of the organization receiving assistance, as described below.

Neighborhood Organizations. CDAs might provide support services for neighborhood organizations by assisting in preparing or duplicating their newsletters or similar mailings. The following examples of support services are from Seattle's Office of Neighborhoods:

Seattle

➤ *Copying service.* Seattle provides a limited amount of copying to help neighborhood organizations conduct neighborhood needs assessments or membership recruitment. Seattle offers to duplicate up to 2,000 copies of one publication per neighborhood organization per year free of charge on a first-come, first-served basis. Neighborhood organizations provide camera-ready copy and the city print shop makes the copies. Seattle has used funds left over from its own printing budget for this and announced the opportunity to neighborhood organizations in its newsletter. Seattle has been able to provide 25-30 neighborhood organizations per year with this service in recent years.

➤ *Resource center.* Seattle's neighborhood resource center is in the Office of Neighborhoods. It is available during regular business hours, but advance arrangements can be made to use it in the evening. It contains neighborhood information, such as neighborhood newsletters and newspapers, neighborhood plans, and books and materials on neighborhood planning, organizing, fundraising.

➤ *Directory of services available.* Seattle's "Whole City Catalog" includes a list of individuals available from various government agencies to provide presentations for neighborhood organizations. These include presentations directly related to neighborhood organization development or interests such as obtaining traffic improvements, establishing a crime watch program, and preserving historic buildings. To compile the catalog, staff sent a memo to department heads asking them to identify presentations they currently provide or could provide.

CDAs may also be able to provide staff support and equipment for some neighborhood organization activities, such as clean-up efforts.

Knoxville

➤ As part of its Operation Community Clean Program, Knoxville provides staff assistance to neighborhood organizations for clean-up days. These are weekend events focused on cleaning up vacant lots and alleys, primarily in low-income areas. CDA staff meet with the neighborhood organizations to explain how the operation works and the responsibilities of the neighborhood organizations and the CDA. The CDA provides: flyers for the neighborhood organizations to distribute to help them recruit volunteers;

trash bags; a banner; and community assistance request forms that volunteers can use to report code violations or other problems noted during the clean-up. CDA staff arrange for dumpsters and trucks to be provided by another city agency, and for the trash to be removed. A CDA staff member is present to supervise during the clean-up, and sometimes other staff participate as volunteers. CDA staff and neighborhood organization leaders walk through the area a few weeks in advance of the clean-up to provide an idea of the scope of the project, and again afterward to see if the project has been satisfactorily completed.

CDAs can also strengthen neighborhood organizations by providing grants for implementing programs or projects. Once neighborhood organizations apply for such grants, however, they are in the same position as any other subgrantee in terms of responsibilities for service provision.

Fairfax County ➤ In Fairfax County, the neighborhood organization in one target area received a grant to provide transportation services for low-income residents in its area. A van had been privately donated to the neighborhood organization, but funds were needed for operating costs. With the grant, the neighborhood organization serves about 60 low- to moderate-income residents per month in a relatively isolated area of the county not served by public transit. The service is limited to necessary trips for shopping, medical appointments, and visits to government offices, with occasional recreational trips for youth groups.

CDAs can also provide mini-grants to encourage neighborhood organizations to initiate small, independent projects as a stepping-stone toward larger projects.

Roanoke ➤ Roanoke offers mini-grants of up to $1,800 (requiring a $1 cash match on the part of the neighborhood organization for every $4 received from the CDA). Mini-grants can be used for implementing neighborhood projects such as beautification efforts and signs, and for activities that support or strengthen the neighborhood organization such as newsletters or rehabilitation of community centers. The CDA provides training workshops in grant administration to help neighborhood organizations succeed with their initial grants, thus encouraging them to implement additional projects.

Small or Minority-Owned Businesses. One way to help support small or minority-owned businesses is by supporting business incubators. Incubators generally provide a combination of low-cost rental space and basic business services such as reception/ clerical staff, photocopying, telephone, telefax, and mail. (Incubators are often made possible through government financial assistance.) Incubators provide the opportunity for tenants to network with and help each other. Some incubators are targeted to businesses owned by minorities, including women; others focus on any small or new businesses. Criteria such as size, income, and age of business should be established for the selection of tenants.

Albany and Rock Island

➤ Albany's CDA provided some of the funds to develop and operate the city's incubator for minority-owned businesses. The incubator is managed by one of the tenants, but CDA staff are involved in oversight. In Rock Island, a CDA staff member manages the incubator, which is funded by the state.

Resources Required To Implement These Ideas

The ideas discussed in this chapter vary considerably in their use of resources. For the most part, staff time is the major resource used for most practices, although some also require printing and distribution of written materials. The most staff time is needed for providing technical assistance and liaisons to neighborhoods. Providing a full-time mediator or ombudsman can also involve substantial staff time, but this is only necessary in very large communities. In most places, such services can be made a part of another position or the CDA might join with other departments to create such a service. Hiring trainers to conduct workshops can be costly, but it may be possible to obtain training services on a volunteer or low-cost basis from community organizations or universities. Providing grants for neighborhood organizations or support for programs such as business incubators requires an allocation of CDA funds.

4

Outreach To Customers

ACTION 4.1 *Market CDA Programs*

    4.1(a)   Use a variety of formats to promote awareness of and support for CDA programs

    4.1(b)   Make special efforts to market programs to minorities

    4.1(c)   Create an identity for community development programs to help make citizens and staff aware of them, and to create team spirit

ACTION 4.2 *Use Neighborhood-Based Outreach Efforts to Encourage Greater Use of Programs by Minorities and Underserved Groups*

ACTION 4.3 *Make Explicit Efforts to be Sensitive to Customers' Needs and Concerns*

    4.3(a)   Promulgate a clear set of organizational values to encourage employees to be sensitive to customers

    4.3(b)   Notify affected residents or businesses in advance of potentially disruptive community development project work in their area such as demolitions and installation of sidewalks and sewers

    4.3(c)   Encourage CDA staff to work as teams to increase responsiveness to customers

    4.3(d)   Provide recognition to citizens for achievements related to CDA goals

    4.3(e)   Encourage staff to be sensitive to the needs of different customers, including minorities

Outreach To Customers

A nother way for CDAs to help customers is through outreach activities. The most common of these is to market CDA programs or activities so as to let potential customers know about the agency's services and programs. Of particular concern are outreach practices to encourage use of CDA programs by customers such as minorities, the homeless, very low income residents, and underserved groups. Encouraging CDA staff sensitivity to clients is another aspect of outreach discussed in this chapter.

ACTION 4.1

Market CDA Programs

(Primary sources: Albany, New York; Cleveland, Ohio; Long Beach, California; Norman, Oklahoma; Roanoke, Virginia; Santa Ana, California)

M arketing of CDA services is needed to ensure that eligible customers use and benefit from CDA services, especially customers in greatest need of them. Marketing can also help build public support for CDA programs that translates into political support for project and budget approval.

Marketing activities include both general and targeted marketing. General marketing to the whole community promotes awareness and support of the CDA's services and programs among the general public. It is also essential to target specific groups that are reluctant to use government services, are less aware of their availability, or are underserved in a particular community. These groups often include minorities or the elderly, among others.

General and targeted marketing overlap. Doing a good job of general marketing is also likely to encourage eligible persons—some of whom belong to targeted customer groups—to apply for specific programs.

4.1(a)   *Use a variety of formats to promote awareness of and support for CDA programs*

Most successful CDAs provide *flyers or brochures* describing specific programs, their eligibility requirements, and application procedures. This should certainly be continued. Many CDAs also produce monthly or quarterly newsletters. These newsletters should contain:

— highlights of various CDA programs, including eligibility and application information;

— information about specific projects, meetings, and workshops;

— "introduction" to CDA staff members;

— articles about activities and progress in various target areas or neighborhoods; and

— information on current city or county events.

CDA staff should develop written materials that are clear, easy-to-understand, and attractive. Graphics are an effective way to draw attention to posters and flyers, for example. Exhibit 4.1 illustrates two different graphics developed by Albany CDA staff for flyers and other announcements used for its paint program. Humor can often help. Exhibit 4.2 shows the use of humorous drawings from Santa Ana's brochure for its rehab loan program. This brochure was printed in color, which also helps attract attention, and was printed in English and Spanish. Developing brochures, flyers, and newsletters is only half the story. Getting them out into the community is what counts. Exhibits 4.3 and 4.4 provide additional suggestions for developing and distributing flyers and brochures.

Exhibit 4.5 provides suggestions for the use of other approaches to marketing such as newspapers, television, and CDA staff personal contacts. Promotional efforts for CDA programs and activities need to be repeated several times during the year. One mailing or one effort at door-to-door distribution of flyers is not sufficient.

A number of CDAs are venturing into use of *videos* for marketing, although *slide presentations*—less expensive but less dramatic—are an effective alternative. Staff members can show videos or slides at meetings of community organizations, at special events where CDAs have booths, at meetings of any groups requesting information on CDA programs, or to introduce CDA activities at meetings held to obtain citizen input for planning or project selection.

Groups such as neighborhood organizations that provide services to target groups, or perhaps religious or social organizations can be asked to show videos or slides to increase awareness of CDA programs.

Videos can be provided to the local public access cable channel, where they can be seen by a broad spectrum of the general public. It

EXHIBIT 4.1

Example of Graphics for Producing Attractive Flyers

THE WEST HILL IMPROVEMENT CORPORATION
PAINT PROGRAM 1990

340 First Street
Albany, NY 12206
Phone: 462-6469

Source: Albany, New York, Department of Housing and Community Development, Flyers used by Neighborhood Improvement Corporations, 1990.

EXHIBIT 4.2

Example of Using Illustrations in Brochures

Low Interest Home Improvement Loans

If your monthly budget is stretched and your home needs remodeling or repairs, here's a sensible answer to your problem. The City of Santa Ana Housing Department has developed a program that enables you to borrow from the equity in your home, at a low interest rate, and pay it back in small monthly payments you can afford.

Start With Our Free Checkup

The program starts with the applicant being financially qualified and then goes on to a free checkup by one of our professional housing experts. Together you will decide what things should be repaired or replaced. Eligible items include anything that may be unhealthy or unsafe in your home such as electrical wiring, plumbing, or leaky roofs. Also included are such things as bedroom additions, an extra bathroom, a new kitchen, interior and exterior painting, and even fences.

After the checkup, we'll give you an estimate of the cost. Then we'll help you obtain the money you need to pay for it.

Préstamos a bajo interes para el mejoramiento de su vivienda

Si su presupuesto mensual no le alcanza para hacer los arreglos necesarios en su casa, nosotros tenemos la solución a su problema. El Departamento de la Vivienda de Santa Ana ha desarrollado un programa que le permite pedir prestado contra el valor contable acumulado en su propiedad a un bajo interes con pequeñas mensualidad.

Comience Con Nuestra Inspeccion Gratuita

El programa se inicia con la aprobación del solicitante si califica economicamente y continúa luego con una inspección gratuita por parte de uno de nuestros expertos profesionales de viviendas. Juntos, Ud. y él decidirán cuales son las cosas que deben ser reparadas o reemplazadas. Las cosas que se pueden considerar son todas aquellas que puedan ser insalubres o peligrosas en su casa, así como conecciones eléctricas, plomería, o techos con goteras o agrietados. También se incluye en este programa la construcción de recámaras adicionales, un baño extra, una cocina nueva, pintura exterior y interior y aún cercos. Después de la inspección, le daremos un costo aproximado. Luego, nosotros le ayudaremos a conseguir el dinero que Ud. necesitará para pagarlo.

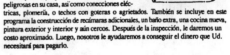

Source: City of Santa Ana, California, Housing Division, "Here's Help to Get Your Home in Shape," 1990.

EXHIBIT 4.3

Suggestions for Flyers and Brochures

Developing Flyers and Brochures

1. Avoid big words and jargon. Explain concepts that may be unfamiliar. For example, a flyer prepared by one of the Albany community organizations explains: "A grant = free money to improve your home." Translate material into the language of non-English speaking minority groups where needed.

2. Use large, easy-to-read typeface to help those with limited vision or limited reading skills.

3. "Consumer test" new materials before mass producing them. Test them on a small sample of clients to determine whether the material is easily understood.

4. Use a customer-friendly format, such as providing information in a question-and-answer form. Try to anticipate the kinds of information customers might want, and express questions and answers in simple terms. For example, what kind of work may be done? Who decides what work is needed? (See exhibit 4.4 for an excerpt from the Norman brochure, which illustrates these points.)

5. Use graphics and illustrations to make printed materials attractive. Color is effective but more expensive.

Distributing Flyers and Brochures

1. Display posters and leave stacks of brochures or flyers at a variety of locations: senior citizen centers, day care centers, health clinics, libraries, community organizations, neighborhood offices of elected officials, and neighborhood stores. Leave information on rehab loans in bank lobbies and real estate offices as well.

2. Mail flyers to each household and homeowner in eligible areas or in areas of the community that are likely to have substantial proportions of eligible homes. Long Beach found it easier to contract to a mailing firm that had collected addresses. The contractor prepared and pasted labels on flyers provided by the agency, at a cost of approximately 12 cents in 1989 for each mailing. For programs aimed at homeowners, Long Beach obtained labels from the assessor's office and sent announcements out itself.

3. Deliver flyers or doorknob hangers door-to-door by using student interns or volunteers from scout troops or other youth organizations.

4. Enclose flyers in utility bills. Albany has enclosed flyers in city water bills.

EXHIBIT 4.4

Example of Providing Information in Customer-Friendly Question and Answer Format

 What Is An Emergency Repair Grant And How Can A Person Qualify For It?

The maximum Emergency Repair Grant limit is $4,000.00. Qualifications for an Emergency Repair Grant are the same as for the Rehabilitation Grant. All properties located within the Corporate City limits of Norman can be eligible for an Emergency Repair Grant. Such funds shall be granted to alleviate harmful conditions in which immediate action is needed and for the following reasons: any act of nature resulting in critical damage to the structural condition, to eliminate specific hazards, or to correct deficiencies in structures which prevent the dwelling from being readily maintainable.

 What Kind Of Work May Be Done?

All work needed to bring the property into compliance with the Standard Housing Code as it pertains to one and two family dwellings. Examples would include repair or replacement of faulty electrical wiring, leaky roofs, and faulty plumbing, as well as removal of open flame or unvented heaters or bad water heaters, etc.

 Who Decides What Work Is Needed?

The Rehabilitation Specialist from the Housing Rehabilitation Office will survey your property and advise you what work must be done.

Source: City of Norman, Oklahoma, Housing Rehabilitation Office, "CDBG Housing Rehabilitation Grant Programs—Common Questions and Answers," 1990.

EXHIBIT 4.5

Suggestions for Marketing Through Other Mechanisms

1. Place ads in local newspapers. Use a variety of community newspapers, including those serving minority and non-English speaking neighborhoods, as well as mainstream newspapers. Long Beach has placed paid ads in neighborhood organization newsletters to get its announcement across and as a way to provide a small amount of financial support to those neighborhood organizations. Long Beach also found the *Penny Saver*, mailed to Long Beach households in specific neighborhoods, to be very effective in getting responses to the city's ads, in part because the mailer was very good at targeting low-income neighborhoods.

2. Use public service announcements on radio and television. Have staff members talk about the program on relevant local radio or television stations, for instance, on home maintenance/repair and small business programs.

3. Use promotional "give-away" items such as key chains or magnifying glasses, the latter being particularly attractive to elderly clients.

4. Seek media coverage by providing press releases on CDA programs and their accomplishments.

5. Inform media about CDA accomplishments. Cleveland provided a bus tour of various CDA projects to 45 reporters, photographers and editors during Community Development Week. The CDA director acted as "tour guide" for the event.

6. Designate a staff member to be a press liaison or public information officer. This person should be the primary contact for media and should be responsible for generating periodic press releases to keep the general public and target audiences aware of CDA programs.

7. Have CDA staff participate in city, county, or neighborhood events. Put up a booth, display and distribute program materials, and have a staff member present to answer questions. Albany has participated in city-sponsored neighborhood street festivals; Cleveland sets up an information booth at its annual home and flower show.

8. Have staff participate in neighborhood activities such as annual clean-up days, when they can talk with potential clients and distribute informational materials.

9. Hold community meetings to introduce new programs in specific areas. Long Beach, for example, usually kicks off each new program in *each* eligible area by holding such a meeting at a school or park in the neighborhood.

10. Use neighborhood meetings to market programs. Long Beach tries to send representatives to most neighborhood organization meetings, to give out flyers sometime during the session.

11. When possible, include the council member representing the district at community meetings sponsored by the CDA. This gives the meeting more prestige and lets the local citizens know that residents' views are important to the government. This is also politically desirable and important to elected officials and will likely increase future program support from these officials.

Exhibit 4.5 (continued)

12. Provide recognition ceremonies for successful neighborhood activities. For example, after a highly successful neighborhood improvement effort, Long Beach sponsored a block party in that neighborhood. A flyer announcing the block party was also used to indicate that funds were still available for the various programs. (See exhibit 4.6.)

13. Have the CDA director and other staff members participate in a government-wide speakers bureau. If there is no such bureau, publicize the availability of CDA staff to speak on topics such as rehab loan programs, obtaining a building permit, code enforcement, and so on to neighborhood organizations, civic groups, and clubs.

may be possible to get them shown on regular broadcast channels as a community service, including channels known to be used by particular CDA target groups, such as Spanish-language stations.

Videos or slides can also be shown to newly elected officials or new CDA staff members to familiarize them with the CDA and what it does.

Norman ➤ Norman CDA staff worked with the local public access channel to produce a video to describe its CDBG services. This channel also ran the video (at no charge) twice a day during the first week it was shown and afterward ran it periodically at the channel's discretion. The CDA received considerable public response to the video in the form of telephone queries and people stopping staff on the street to ask questions.

Roanoke ➤ Roanoke produced a television program on the community planning process. Staff used a shortened version of it at the opening of meetings held to obtain citizen input for neighborhood plans.

Following are some recommendations for developing videos:

❒ First decide who your target audience is and what message you want to get across. Include materials likely to register with the target audience, such as before and after views of houses that have been rehabilitated, or footage showing customers going through the application process. Try to include as many "action" segments as possible. Try to use a non-bureaucratic touch and some humor, if possible. Include brief interviews with residents whose homes have been rehabilitated under CDA programs, as done in Norman.

❒ Make videos brief (about 15 minutes) to hold attention without boring an audience.

EXHIBIT 4.6

Example of Recognition Event Publicity

NEIGHBORHOOD BLOCK PARTY

Join Us! Saturday, May 20th
Lime Avenue
(between 21st & Hill)
10:00 A.M.–2:00 P.M.

Free Food & Drinks

Drawing for Free Prizes   *Music*

The Community Development Department invites you to attend a block party in recognition of you and your neighbors participation in Neighborhood Improvement and clean up efforts in the Atlantic/King Park Area. Join Councilman Clarence Smith in this celebration of civic pride and discover more about Neighborhood Improvement Programs.

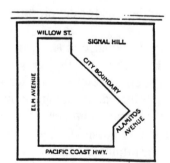

There are funds *still* available for you to:

- Receive up to $2,000 to improve the exterior of your property.

- Receive up to $500 worth of free tool rental assistance.

- Borrow up to $25,000 to fix up your home at 3%, 6%, or 8% interest, some with no monthly payments.

- Borrow up to $5,000 per unit at 4% interest for rehabilitating rental property.

- Get graffiti removed from your property absolutely free.

Source: Long Beach , California, Community Development Department, 1989.

❏ Rehearse interviews and other speaking segments before taping videos. Keep speaking segments short unless accompanied by more exciting visuals. Allocate time to think about and arrange for backdrops or location sites. Include background music. These measures will help create a video with a more polished, professional look.

❏ Use experienced personnel to create the video. Seek advice and help from such persons as staff of the local public access channel, or from faculty members in communications or television production at a nearby college or university, or seek paid professional help, if funds are available.

The major drawback to videos is that they can require considerable time commitment and often financial commitment for planning and preparation. Tasks include designing the content of the video, developing the script, and lining up participants. Video production can involve many hours for taping time and for editing and splicing the video, not all of which involves CDA staff.

CDAs should monitor responses to various kinds of promotional efforts to find out which ones work best. This can be done by including a "how did you hear about this program" question on application forms, or by having staff ask that question when potential clients call to ask about programs.

4.1(b)   *Make special efforts to market programs to minorities*

The following are suggestions for targeting marketing efforts to minority clients.

❏ Advertise in, and send press releases to, minority newspapers and minority-focused radio stations.

Albany ➤ Albany's CDA provides 50 percent of the operating costs of the local nonprofit minority newspaper, which is available free of charge at locations such as stores, commercial or public buildings and nonprofit organizations in minority neighborhoods. For this financial support, the paper provides two pages of space to the CDA at no charge for CDA program articles or advertising.

❏ Translate flyers, other announcements, and advertisements into minority languages. This is particularly advisable for programs targeted to neighborhoods with substantial numbers of foreign-language speakers.

❏ Advertise through minority organization fundraising events (charity dances or dinners) or newsletters.

❏ Post notices and leave brochures or flyers in heavily utilized locations in minority neighborhoods such as community centers, day care centers, government or nonprofit organization offices, libraries, and recreation facilities. Contact minority churches and social organizations to see about posting announcements and leaving brochures.

❏ Identify active minority community groups and tap into their networks.

Long Beach ➤ Long Beach has worked with Cambodian monks, Vietnamese business people, black churches and Hispanic social clubs to publicize CDA programs to minority groups.

❏ For programs targeted at minority businesses, post and leave brochures or flyers in adult education institutions with large minority enrollment such as trade or vocational education schools or community colleges. Contact minority sub-groups of the Chamber of Commerce and any other minority business-oriented group to leave informational material or have staff make presentations. Leave announcements regarding bidding opportunities (such as for housing rehab work) at the stores of suppliers likely to be used by minority contractors.

4.1(c) *Create an identity for community development programs to help make citizens and staff aware of them and to create team spirit*

Simple techniques, such as use of a slogan, specially designed T-shirts, buttons and banners can promote particular programs and foster a sense of belonging among customers and staff. Building team spirit encourages greater use of CDA programs and more citizen participation.

Norman ➤ Norman made special efforts to develop an identity for the residents of each of its target neighborhoods through use of color-coded printed materials, buttons, and banners. Announcements for the two annual neighborhood meetings (where citizen input for CDBG projects is sought) were printed in a different color for each neighborhood. The CDA prepared buttons in the same colors for residents of those areas to wear at meetings of the policy committee and at the city council hearing on the CDBG budget. The buttons displayed a drawing of the type of housing typical for that neighborhood and the name of the neighborhood. (See exhibit 4.7.)

Norman ➤ A Norman CDA staff member has been designing a T-shirt each year since 1987. T-shirts are sold for $8-$10 to citizens who want them, primarily to those active in target areas. Staff and citizens are often stopped and asked about their T-shirts. This provides an opportunity to explain the program and to encourage people to contact the office for more information. Thus, the shirts can help recruit potential customers, particularly when worn in target areas.

T-shirts can be self-supporting, as indicated above. Producing buttons and banners need not be expensive. Norman was able to borrow a button-making machine, so only had to pay for material to make the buttons (about $160 to make 1,000 buttons). The drawings for the buttons were done by a CDA staff member. Small banners with the neighborhood's name printed on it—displayed at meetings and hearings—cost approximately $25-$30 each.

ACTION 4.2

Use Neighborhood-Based Outreach Efforts To Encourage Greater Use of Programs by Minorities and Underserved Groups

(Primary sources: Albany, New York; Long Beach, California)

Some potential clients are reluctant to go to offices that are in unfamiliar locations or are difficult to reach. Travel is a hardship for some low-income and elderly people. Some low-income or minority clients may be reluctant to deal with government agencies or provide information to government officials who may be perceived as not understanding their concerns.

Explicit neighborhood-based outreach in minority neighborhoods or those with underserved groups can help alleviate these problems. These approaches include:

— Establishing neighborhood offices of the CDA in target areas, including minority communities or areas where minority businesses are concentrated;

EXHIBIT 4.7

Example of Buttons Used to Create "Team Spirit" Among Residents in Target Neighborhoods

Source: Norman, Oklahoma, Planning Department, 1990.

— Contracting with neighborhood organizations in these areas to promote programs and, perhaps, to perform intake functions such as screening applicants and helping them prepare application forms. Such arrangements can also be made with community leaders or residents who are particularly active in the community. These approaches may be particularly helpful for such programs as housing or business rehabilitation, weatherization, or paint programs;

— Establishing advisory boards with full representation of minorities to obtain input and advice about developing and marketing programs, particularly minority-oriented programs.

The convenience of *neighborhood offices* encourages clients to drop in to find out about and apply for programs. Neighborhood offices are also likely to be perceived as friendlier and less intimidating than government office buildings because they are in the neighborhood and because they are likely to be storefront offices or houses converted into offices. They also offer opportunities to reach minorities.

Long Beach ➤ Long Beach opened a neighborhood storefront for programs in the city's major distressed commercial/residential area. The office is initially focusing on encouraging local businesses to apply for rehabilitation funds. The site chosen for the CDA's storefront office is being rehabilitated, thus the office itself will serve as a demonstration of the program's results.

Albany ➤ Albany houses two minority-focused programs in its minority business incubator. This provides easy access to a variety of related services. Customers who come to the incubator for one service are frequently referred to another service while they are there.

Using neighborhood organizations or residents to market CDA programs can also lead to greater use of programs. Some customers—particularly low-income or minority customers—are likely to feel more comfortable dealing with such individuals than with the CDA. For example, neighborhood organization staff, community activists, and residents are likely to be familiar to customers because they are often out and around in the neighborhood in conjunction with various activities, or because they live in the neighborhood they serve. Neighborhood organization personnel are also likely to be familiar with neighborhood concerns and be comfortable dealing with neighborhood residents. Thus, potential clients for CDA programs are likely to perceive these individuals as being on their side.

Albany   ➤   Albany's CDA has contracts with four Neighborhood Improvement Corporations (NICs) to perform marketing and client screening and intake for residential rehab loans and emergency assistance grants. Albany's contract stipulates that one or more of the three NIC staff live in the neighborhood. NIC staff report that customers find neighborhood offices more convenient than the CDA office. CDA staff find it helpful to use neighborhood organizations because some citizens are not comfortable borrowing from the government.

Long Beach   ➤   Long Beach hired as a consultant one resident activist who had had success with a home rehabilitation grant. The agency asked her to visit each household in her neighborhood—one of the most distressed neighborhoods in the city—to encourage other households to have their homes rehabilitated. Most of the homeowners have since rehabilitated their homes either through the agency program or on their own. The agency has since used her to help market other programs as well. The agency had such success with this that they have begun to look for individuals in other neighborhoods who can be similarly employed. The agency uses a form of consultant contract to give them control over the process.

CDAs, however, should provide advice and/or assistance to neighborhood organizations or individuals for their marketing efforts. CDAs might consider providing occasional marketing seminars or workshops for neighborhood organization personnel led by marketing or advertising professionals. Marketing professors at local universities or staff of local businesses might be willing to lead such seminars or provide one-on-one advice on a voluntary or low-cost basis. CDAs can also call occasional meetings to encourage neighborhood organizations to exchange marketing/outreach ideas and experiences.

Albany   ➤   Albany provides marketing advice and assistance to Neighborhood Improvement Corporations in several ways. Marketing ideas are brainstormed during a monthly meeting between CDA staff and the NIC director. The CDA also reimburses NICs for marketing materials they develop, as well as providing brochures and flyers for them to distribute. CDA staff and computer capabilities have been used to develop NIC flyers and brochures. The program compliance officer also informally makes marketing suggestions during monthly site visits.

CDAs can also provide marketing assistance by providing information to help neighborhood organizations target potential clients.

In Albany, the CDA provided lists of homeowners from tax roles and lists of housing code violators to enable NICs to target mailings for the rehab loan program.

Advisory board members can help "get the word out" about CDA programs to the minority community, can serve as a sounding board for ideas, and as a way for CDAs to touch base with reality in the minority community. This can help staff avoid potential blunders based on lack of familiarity with minority groups, especially those from other countries.

Resources required. Although contracting arrangements for outreach require the CDA to pay for services, this may simply involve having non-staff personnel perform outreach activities that would otherwise be done by CDA staff. Thus, this kind of arrangement may not always represent any extra cost to the CDA. It may also be possible to make similar outreach arrangements using volunteers.

ACTION 4.3

> ## *Make Explicit Efforts to be Sensitive to Customers' Needs and Concerns*
>
> (Primary Sources: Albany, New York; Austin, Texas; Cleveland, Ohio; Long Beach, California; Lower Merion Township, Pennsylvania; San Mateo County, California)

The "actions" discussed here and in chapters 2 and 3 all promote closeness to customers. CDAs that use practices such as obtaining input from citizens affected by a project or making extra efforts to ensure that clients are aware of warranty provisions are, in effect, encouraging staff to be sensitive to customers.

In addition, however, CDA managers should encourage an atmosphere of sensitivity and service to the customer. Managers should urge their staff to continually "put themselves in the customers' shoes."

4.3(a)   *Promulgate a clear set of organizational values to encourage employees to be sensitive to customers*

Austin   ➤ In Austin, Texas, the mayor and city council made improving the quality of customer service one of their top priorities for 1990. A city-wide program called BASICS (Building Austin's Standards for Customer Service) was introduced, and the city manager established a task force to design a comprehensive plan for improving customer service. One aspect of this effort is training in customer sensitivity for employees. While this was a city-wide effort, CDAs could introduce a "mini-program" for their own staff.

4.3(b) *Notify affected residents or businesses in advance of potentially disruptive community development project work in their area such as demolitions and installation of sidewalks and sewers*

Chapter 2 suggested advance notifications to give residents and businesses the opportunity to speak out about work that will affect them. Here the emphasis is on ensuring that they are aware of such work and can make any needed preparations.

Putting flyers under doors or using doorknob hangers in the area where work will take place at least one week, and preferably two, in advance of the project activity will give citizens time to indicate any concerns and to adjust any affected activities. When preparing such notifications, include the nature of the activity that will take place; the reason for the activity and how long the project work will take; the dates during which work will be done; and a telephone number and name to contact in case this poses any special problem or the resident has any questions.

4.3(c) *Encourage CDA staff to work as teams to increase responsiveness to customers*

Team members should keep each other informed about the status of projects, ensuring that more than one staff member is able to handle calls from clients, as done in Lower Merion Township and San Mateo County (see chapter 5).

4.3(d) *Provide recognition to citizens for achievements related to CDA goals*

Consider giving awards or certificates, or holding recognition events such as ceremonies or block parties. CDAs should also encourage neighborhood organizations and the corporate community to provide or fund such recognition.

Recognition should not be limited to citizens who have worked on specific CDA or community programs, but should extend to citizens who have had other accomplishments related to CDA goals such as excellent property maintenance. Such gestures of appreciation will increase morale in the neighborhood and encourage future activity.

Long Beach ➤ Long Beach sponsored a block party in a neighborhood that had completed a highly successful improvement effort. The CDA provided the dollars for the activity, while residents staffed the effort. (See exhibit 4.6 for the party announcement.)

Cleveland ➤ As part of Cleveland's code enforcement partnership, homeowners whose homes do not have any code violations or who correct their violations are given a certificate for outstanding property maintenance (exhibit 4.8). The certificate is signed by the mayor, the CDA director and other officials, and presented at a regular neighborhood organization meeting to which neighborhood residents are invited. Staff find that recipients of certificates frequently become volunteers for the code enforcement program (see chapter 7).

4.3(e) *Encourage staff to be sensitive to the needs of different customers, including minorities*

CDA clients can vary greatly. Differences in language, age, race/ethnicity, education, technical acumen, and familiarity with government programs should be considered and reflected in agency activities. Staff will need to exercise considerable patience in dealing with the elderly, the less educated, and those with limited English-language ability.

One way to promote staff sensitivity is to provide them training in customer sensitivity and customer service.

Austin ➤ The City of Austin provided training opportunities as part of a city-wide focus on improved customer service (see Action 4.3(a)). Training was provided for approximately 1,400 supervisors and managers at a day-long conference during customer service week. Topics included training employees to be customer-friendly and to respond nicely to customers in writing, to deal with unhappy customers, to serve customers with disabilities, and to emphasize quality performance. Training sessions were videotaped so they could be viewed by all employees on the city's public access cable channel or by borrowing the tapes from the city's collection of customer service materials.

EXHIBIT 4.8

Example of Citizen Recognition Award Certificate For Property Maintenance

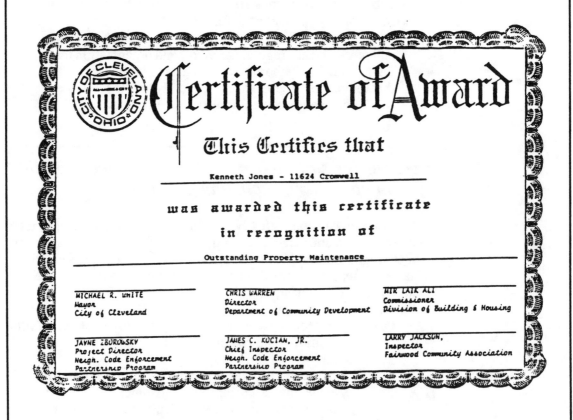

Source: Cleveland, Ohio, Department of Community Development, Neighborhood Code Enforcement Partnership Program, 1990.

San Mateo County ➤ CDA staff in San Mateo County participated in a county-sponsored workshop on "Dealing with Difficult People." The workshop taught how to work with people whose values and attitudes differ from yours. Although the workshop was intended to provide guidance in dealing with the public, staff members also found it helped them work with other employees.

CDA managers can also promote sensitivity to customers by discussing this topic at regular staff meetings, which shows that management takes this issue very seriously. Staff can be asked for ideas for improvement and teams of employees can be delegated to implement these improvements in CDA customer service operations.

If feasible, establish a staff position or part of a position for a minority affairs officer to coordinate, advise on, and assist in implementing minority-focused programs, as done in Albany. The person acts as a mediator when necessary and serves as a general liaison to the minority community.

If some minority groups do not speak English as their primary language, have staff members who speak their language and are familiar with their culture serve as a liaison to them. If this is not possible, arrange for a translator to work with and advise staff.

Provide staff with skills and experience that will fit the needs of minority customers. For example, staff involved with programs of interest to minority businesses should be sensitized to, and informed about, minority business concerns.

Resources Required to Implement These Ideas

The time and cost of the practices described in this chapter vary considerably. Staff time is the primary resource needed for practices related to closeness to customers. Costs related to advertising and development and distribution of promotional materials are also involved. For both costs, however, the CDA has considerable flexibility in designing these programs to accommodate its resource constraints.

In any case, most of the basic actions suggested in this chapter should be considered by the CDA as inherent parts of its work, not as additional workload for staff.

5

Encouraging Employee Involvement

ACTION 5.1 *Build Teams and a Spirit of Teamwork*

  5.1(a) Develop a clear set of organizational values that emphasize the importance of teamwork

  5.1(b) Use teams with increased employee responsibility and autonomy to deliver services

  5.1(c) Use teams to examine work processes in order to streamline and improve service quality

  5.1(d) Schedule employee involvement events throughout the year

  5.1(e) Use informal procedures to create a sense of team and group identity

ACTION 5.2 *Communicate Frequently and Listen Effectively to Employees*

  5.2(a) Be available to speak with staff

  5.2(b) Visit workers in the field

  5.2(c) Conduct annual or semi-annual retreats

  5.2(d) Hold regularly scheduled staff meetings

  5.2(e) Survey employees periodically

  5.2(f) Look for ways to enhance existing opportunities to communicate informally with staff

ACTION 5.3 *Encourage Genuine Staff Participation in Decision Making*

ACTION 5.4   *Provide Incentives for Improved Performance*

   5.4(a)   Use a variety of mechanisms to recognize employee contributions

   5.4(b)   Increase employee responsibility to encourage good performance

ACTION 5.5   *Train Employees*

   5.5(a)   Conduct periodic assessments of agency personnel training needs

   5.5(b)   Provide cross training

   5.5(c)   Measure training effectiveness

   5.5(d)   Train management and staff in new processes or procedures

Encouraging Employee Involvement

To fulfill the CDA's mission, the people who are directly providing the service—the employees—need to be given responsibility and authority to act. They should be involved in the everyday decisions. The manner in which employees carry out their duties, to a large extent, determines the success of the agency.

How CDA employees think of themselves and the degree to which they are involved in their work are reflected in the way they treat clients. If a CDA applies a lower standard for treating employees than clients, employees feel less motivated, less enthusiastic, and less inclined to provide superior service. Involved employees are better equipped to think on their feet and to react faster and more spontaneously to service demands and changes in the environment. Also, involvement leads to a greater sense of pride and ownership in the mission and purpose of the organization.

This chapter describes several approaches that CDA employers can use to encourage employee involvement. The key for widespread, long-term success is to use a variety of methods. Rarely will any one approach be sufficient.

ACTION 5.1

Build Teams and a Spirit of Teamwork
(Primary sources: Long Beach, California; Santa Ana, California; San Mateo County, California; Lower Merion Township, Pennsylvania)

This approach applies both to the whole agency and to groups of small teams formed on a continuing or ad hoc basic to accomplish specific tasks.

5.1(a) *Develop clear organizational values that emphasize the importance of teamwork*

Having a set of shared beliefs or values on which to base a series of organizational changes provides an important stepping stone to success. The very process of involving employees in the identification of basic organizational values can contribute immeasurably to building effective teams. Staff often resent being told how to do something. Their involvement in identifying the purpose behind an action can neutralize or reverse their resentment and lack of interest. Employee task forces and staff/management groups can be used to develop and clarify an organization's values. Each CDA should have a set of written out staff-developed values. See exhibit 5.1 for an example from Long Beach, California.

One of the advantages of having a value statement is that it sets a tone for future changes that are consistent with the values. One disadvantage is that a lack of consistency in applying the spirit of the values may lead to low morale and employee discouragement. Thus, the obvious challenge is to live up to the articulated values.

5.1(b) *Use teams with increased employee responsibility and autonomy to deliver services*

CDAs should deploy work teams with increased responsibility and autonomy for providing direct service to the public. In addition to improving communications among team members, this approach improves customer service and employee performance, as exemplified in San Mateo County and Lower Merion Township.

San Mateo County ➤ The San Mateo County CDA "Matrix Management System" organizes rehab specialists into two-person teams responsible for specific target areas. Team members stay knowledgeable and keep each other informed about the client and the rehab projects in their areas so either can respond to questions or requests if the other is not available. Both rehab specialists participate in an initial survey of the house and meet the client. This also allows the survey to be done faster—in 45 minutes as opposed to an hour and a half if one person were doing it. The client is told that either of the specialists can be contacted if problems arise. One team member plays a lead role per project, and at least weekly, each specialist visits projects for which the other is leader to see what kind of progress has been made. The team keeps a joint calendar to avoid duplication of efforts.

EXHIBIT 5.1

Example of a Set of Organizational Values

The
City of
LongBeach

WHAT WE BELIEVE
THE CITY'S BUSINESS IS SERVICE

We are committed to providing quality service to our diverse community in ways that are helpful, caring, and responsive.

WORKING TOGETHER TO SERVE

We believe that the success of our organization depends on teamwork, mutual trust, and honesty achieved through commitment to the following values:

Participation by citizens and City team members in setting and attaining the City's goals. **Communication** with one another and with citizens. **Courtesy** in all personal relations. **Integrity** in everything we do. **Loyalty** to our community, to this organization, and to each team member. **Innovation** in meeting the present and future needs of the City. **Responsibility** as a team for the efficient and effective delivery of services. **Pride** in our work, in our dedication to public service, and in being the best we can be.

Source: Long Beach, California, back of business card, 1990.

Lower Merion Township ➤ In Lower Merion Township, a very small agency, all four persons are responsible for services and each tries to stay knowledgeable about all their customers. The director, planner, rehab specialist, and administrative assistant/secretary all know where the appropriate records are filed, are aware of problem cases, and can quickly determine the status of the project for clients who call or write in.

5.1(c) *Use teams to examine work processes in order to streamline and improve service quality*

Involving employees in improving organization productivity not only builds morale but also takes advantage of the firsthand knowledge of staff and provides them a fuller picture of the service/program in which they are working. All of this should lead to more responsive service to the public.

Exhibit 5.2 describes steps to forming successful problem-solving teams. These are based on the experience of Santa Ana, which established quality teams using as a model the Edwards Deming quality management process. (See Action 7.3, chapter 7 for a specific example from Santa Ana of a team's examining its housing rehab loan process.)

Problem-solving teams have the following *benefits:*

— Teams create a sense of unity and group bonding among the members.

— Productivity gains are promoted because the big picture allows team members to become more creative, innovative, and to take more risks, all of which should lead to improved public service. For example, the Santa Ana team reduced the amount of time to process a loan from 71 to 38 days. Not only did this benefit the customers, it also instilled a sense of pride in the employee.

— Customer relations can improve because training and the team process itself emphasize customer service and an understanding of the customer's needs and problems.

Problem-solving work teams have the following potential *obstacles and problems*:

— The extensive amount of training may be viewed by some staff as unnecessarily long and detracting from other important duties and responsibilities.

EXHIBIT 5.2

Forming Problem-Solving Teams

A team generally should be composed of non-supervisory personnel who belong to the work group concerned with the process being examined.

1. *Provide team training.* Santa Ana team members were given 20 half-day training sessions on how to systematically examine work problems. It is important to include *all* team members in this training. Subjects addressed were:

    — Enhancing interpersonal communications skills;

    — "Flow-charting" the sequence of the process;

    — Analyzing the process through basic statistical analysis, including random sampling;

    — Identifying problems in the current process;

    — Brainstorming to identify options for improvement;

    — Gathering data needed to analyze the various options;

    — Using customer and employee surveys;

    — Conducting effective meetings;

    — Effective listening;

    — Analyzing the data to assess each option, including cost and effectiveness analysis;

    — Recommending changes to management for the items the quality team cannot change on its own; and

    — Monitoring the changes to determine if they work.

    This training will initially have to be obtained from outside the agency. Eventually, agency personnel may be able to take over.

2. *Implement the team process.* The team should meet about twice a month, and should select a facilitator and recorder at one of its early meetings. These tasks can be rotated. The skill of the facilitator in relaxing participants, getting them to contribute freely, and helping people resolve differences is a key to continued success.

    The facilitator or recorder should prepare an agenda based on progress at the previous meeting and any ideas that may have arisen since then. The agenda should be distributed at least a day prior to the meeting.

(continued)

Exhibit 5.2 (continued)

If the team does not have immediate consensus on which issue to tackle, it will need to brainstorm to develop a lengthy list from which to choose the priority topic. As its first project, the Santa Ana team chose to study the processing time from initial loan application to loan approval.

3. *Systematically analyze the problem being examined.* The team should use techniques it learned in training sessions to: outline the work steps involved in the problem/issue the team is examining; list the key problem elements in the current process; identify options for correcting the problem; estimate the cost and likely benefits of each option; and select the option to be implemented.

4. *Make recommendations to management and implement those approved.* The team will need to make its recommendations in writing and orally. It should brief each manager concerned on the team's findings and recommendation. Each layer of management should be given the opportunity to question and object to or approve each recommendation.

5. *Provide continued analysis and improvement.* The team should continue to monitor the process examined, collecting and reexamining data that indicates whether its recommendations are working. For example, Santa Ana monitored data on loan processing times on a monthly basis. Once satisfied that times had been reduced, the team revisited its original list to select another problem to work on.

— The problem-solving process tends to require a fair amount of basic statistics, which may be difficult for some employees to grasp and may discourage them.

— Team members may encounter difficulty communicating with those who have not been through the special training, employees who feel left out of the "new" way of thinking about one's job.

— Sustaining long-term team efforts is often difficult for organizations that must deal with the pressures of day-to-day problems. Sustaining enthusiasm and interest requires managers and workers to become fully comfortable with the team process and to provide work time for teams to meet regularly to develop recommendations.

— Use of non-management teams to suggest improvements may be unfamiliar and threatening to some managers. This problem can be alleviated by encouraging discussion among managers on the pros and cons of forming problem-solving work teams *before* the process is implemented; by providing opportunities for all managers to receiving training in the techniques in which the non-management team members will be trained, as done in Santa Ana for the city manager and major department heads; and by having upper management indicate to managers its support of the group process.

Problem-solving work teams are appropriate for all but the smallest CDAs, which are already likely to be working like teams anyway. Teams are likely to be successful if they have full, active management support and workers see advantages in participating. Heavy-handed pressure from upper-level management to force the process is unlikely to be successful.

5.1(d)   *Schedule employee involvement events throughout the year*

Employee involvement should not be seen as a one-time event but as multiple events where employees and managers get together both formally and informally throughout the year to promote and empha-size the team concept. Exhibit 5.3 lists a number of such events.

In promoting team concept, what managers do and how they do it are far more important than what they say. If managers only socialize with other managers, the "we-are-all-in-it-together" con-cept is hard to implement with the rank and file. Leaders and man-agers need to interact informally and frequently with staff.

Develop a range of events such as holiday gatherings, staff lunches, or departmental breakfasts at which managers recognize good group or individual performance, and present customer letters of recognition.

Publish a schedule in advance so employees can choose from a number of different events. A schedule also represents a fixed, visible commitment on the part of the organization. Whether or not people choose to participate, just the fact that the schedule is there contrib-utes to the team concept.

Long Beach   ➢ Long Beach, California, holds monthly breakfasts in a library building adjacent to the CDA office. Participation is voluntary; food and drink are provided on a potluck basis and the atmosphere is quite informal. Responsibility for the food, room set-up, and clean-up is rotated among CDA programs. At the event, the CDA director announces awards for suggestions, introduces new hires, and acknowledges promotions. At times, "Happy Birthday" is sung to staff with recent birthdays.

EXHIBIT 5.3

Examples of Employee Involvement Events

---

1. Monthly all-staff meetings.

2. Monthly division meetings.

3. Weekly/bi-weekly first-line group meetings.

4. Meal get-togethers at breakfast or lunch.

5. Awards and recognition ceremonies.

6. Manager "walk-abouts"—visiting each unit and talking with staff.

7. Bus "ride-arounds" for all staff, to visit major CDA work sites and be briefed by relevant staff about each site.

8. Agency picnics.

Note: Items 1-3 and 6 are discussed in more detail under Action 5.2; item 5 under Action 5.4.

Knoxville ➤ Knoxville, Tennessee borrowed a bus from the city parks and recreation department to take all staff (blue-collar, white-collar, secretarial, and professional staff) on a half-day visit to key work sites such as downtown beautification projects, city redevelopment areas, housing rehab sites, and non-profit service facilities that had been supported by CDA programs. Staff used the bus microphone to brief staff on individual sites. This gave staff members a chance to interact between stops, and to obtain a better overall picture of CDA-wide projects.

Obstacles or Concerns

Events, such as breakfasts, picnics, and bus tours, require staff time to organize and can take away from regular work time. Attendance, especially if it overlaps with the work day, can put an added burden on employees that do not attend or put staff behind on their other work. On the other hand, for these events to work, not all of them can be scheduled after hours.

It is hard to measure the tangible outcomes of such organizational events. What is clear is that employees respond positively when they are treated with respect as individuals in a pleasant and supportive environment. When employees see their managers go out of their way to listen, get involved, and provide recognition and informal pats on the back, they are more willing to do the same with one another and the people they serve.

5.1(e) *Use informal procedures to create a sense of team and group identity*

Team T-shirts, buttons, office decorations, and work unit sponsorship of sports teams can help forge and create a sense of staff involvement and team identity. However, merely giving a worker a personalized coffee mug with the name of the organization on it will not compel the worker to identify with the organization. But these small tangible techniques do have their place as a *supplemental* approach toward reinforcing the concept of team identity.

It is amazing what people will do for an inexpensive T-shirt if there is an explicit importance behind it. For example, there are people who will run a marathon and proudly wear a T-shirt from that race because it represents a significant accomplishment.

Norman ➤ In Norman, Oklahoma, the staff was very proud that each year the CDA sponsored a contest to redesign the CDBG T-shirt to reflect the organization.

San Mateo County ➤ Rather than using titles and full names on internal documents and staff reports, San Mateo County, California refers to all staff, including the director, by first name only—a practice consistent with the matrix management system in San Mateo.

ACTION 5.2

Communicate Frequently and Listen Effectively to Employees

(Primary Sources: San Mateo County, California; Long Beach, California; Knoxville, Tennessee; King County, Washington)

Employees need frequent opportunities to share their views and ideas, and managers, in turn, need to respond. Actively engaging in communications on a regular basis is built into many of the ideas contained in the previous team building section of this chapter.

Communication is much more than merely directing and informing employees. Successful communication is a two-way process that, in some cases, will require managers to practice their listening techniques.

For example, in Knoxville it is part of the organizational culture to offer daily encouragement to the staff to provide input. It is important for managers to sustain this kind of activity, but to a considerable extent this depends on the attitude of the individual managers rather than on any specific action.

The following are ideas for frequently communicating with and effectively listening to employees.

5.2(a) *Be available to speak with staff*

San Mateo County ➤ In San Mateo County, the CDA director established an open-door policy to ensure that any employee may make an appointment and be heard on any issue. Her pledge to the staff is that she will listen and turn away no one. Whether or not she takes action on what she hears still remains her prerogative. Any open-door policy can be established by setting aside specific blocks of unstructured time during the week for drop-in visits by staff. The employee just has to call ahead and reserve 15 minutes. The leader guarantees to be in the office, available to chat.

King County ➤ In King County, the CDA director scheduled a set time each week to meet informally with staff after working hours in a local cafe.

Long Beach ➤ The Long Beach CDA director scheduled a series of events throughout the year to create opportunities not only to communicate with staff and recognize employee contributions, but also to listen to what was on the minds of anybody who happened to be at that event. During the breakfast meeting, for example, people at all levels in the organization felt comfortable approaching the director with questions or items to discuss.

5.2(b) *Visit workers in the field*

"Manager walk-about," what Tom Peters called "Management by Wandering Around," provides the leader the opportunity to listen to and communicate with workers on their turf. This action sends a clear message to the staff that they are important enough for their leaders to come to them.

Knoxville ➤ The Knoxville director has periodically spent time in the field with crews responsible for clean-up, mowing of lots, and demolitions. (The crew members felt that, along with their participation in other activities, this was the first time upper management had expressed such interest in their work and was visibly seen on-site.)

5.2(c)   *Conduct annual or semi-annual retreats*

A sign of a healthy organization is its ability to step back from busy activities, remove staff from the pressures of daily decision making, and reflect on where the organization is going and how to get there. Staff retreats are a prime way to do this. They can also clear the air, provide a better understanding of what the director wants, and promote team spirit. A well-planned retreat can be especially useful if the agency has been having communication or morale problems.

Retreats can also be used for specific purposes such as working on the agency's annual work plan and budget, discussed further under Action 5.3.

Long Beach ➤ In Long Beach, the CDA director used a managerial retreat to begin the team-building process after she took over the responsibility of the department. Prior to the event a committee of managers was formed to help develop the retreat ground rules, identify concerns and develop retreat objectives, and prepare the agenda. The committee also participated in the selection of a professional facilitator, who interviewed each manager and the director and had each participant complete a questionnaire. The interviews and questionnaire helped the agency develop a clearer picture of the participants' expectation. The findings of the questionnaire were provided to the management team. The two-day retreat was held off-site at a park facility. Meals were provided, and an informal casual atmosphere was encouraged.

An action plan based on the retreat discussions was later developed and disseminated. Two divisions have already conducted similar retreats on their own, modeling the format on the managers' retreat.

Knoxvile ➤ Knoxville conducts an annual two-day all staff retreat away from the office to discuss problems, undertake program planning, and help develop the agency's annual action plan. At the first retreat, codes enforcement staff identified too much time spent in paperwork, too many repeat offenders, and a huge backlog of condemned houses to be demolished as major impediments to their productivity. Through employee teams they have now substantially reduced each of these problems; for example, by flow-charting their operations and reducing paperwork to one computer-integrated complaint card. They developed an environmental court for repeat offenders, where offenders have been fined as much as $4,400. The demolition crew did a cost/benefit analysis to prove that the purchase of new demolition equipment would more than pay for itself and eliminate the backlog of condemned houses. The results: a 108 percent increase in number of annual inspections completed, a 400 percent improvement in one-day response time to complaints, elimination of the backlog of condemned houses to be demolished, and a 375 percent increase in the number of condemned houses demolished each year.

See exhibit 5.4 for suggestions for setting up a retreat.

5.2(d) *Hold regularly scheduled staff meetings*

Regular staff meetings held at least monthly for all agency personnel is a way to communicate across divisions, provide recognition to meritorious employees, and permit the discussion of agency-wide issues. Lower-level managers, down to first-line supervisors, might also hold some meetings with their staff. Knoxville and San Mateo County applied this approach to improving communication and providing opportunities for management to *listen* to employees. The following are elements that should be considered regarding staff meetings:

— Meetings should be scheduled at a regular time each month, allowing personnel to fit them more easily into their schedules. Meetings should be not longer than an hour.

— Employees should be encouraged to attend, but attendance should not be mandatory. There are many reasons why people may not be able to participate in a particular meeting.

EXHIBIT 5.4

Retreat Implementation Suggestions

The following are some issues to consider when launching an annual retreat, whether it includes all staff, only managers, or only employees from any one section.

Where should the retreat be held? Get away from the office and the telephone. Some agencies have used sites outside of town, others have used city facilities away from city hall. One option might be to utilize the facilities of another government entity. An outside setting of a retreat is likely to provide an uninterrupted and more relaxed atmosphere and enhance the willingness of people to come up with new ideas.

How long should the retreat be? This depends on the agenda. However, one day is likely to be too short for large agencies, particularly if the goal is to undertake a project during the retreat, such as the preparation of an action plan for the year. Also, one day does not offer the opportunity for the group to get out of its routine and develop more creative, spontaneous working relations.

Should the retreat be an overnight event? Going away overnight provides social and informal time for the participants to get to know each other better. The disadvantage, in addition to cost, is inconvenience, especially for those with family obligations. Whether or not the retreat is overnight, the CDA should try to build in social, informal, unstructured time to allow for small group activities such as sports, dining together, chatting, playing games, or taking walks.

Should the format be structured? There should be opportunity for both structured discussion and small group activity. Small groups provide the opportunity for everyone to participate. Small group findings can then be brought back to the larger group.

Should an outside facilitator be used? The use of a facilitator is generally recommended when a group has had little experience working together. The facilitator is an unemotional, neutral party who can help the group meet its objectives. Of the three examples in this section, Long Beach and Knoxville used outside facilitators; King County did not.

Who should plan the retreat? Whatever mechanism is used to set the agenda, participants should feel they have been given an opportunity to participate in planning the agenda and tone. One way is for a facilitator to get staff input before developing the agenda, as was done in Long Beach. Another way is to form a small committee to do the interviewing and develop the agenda.

What role should leadership play in the retreat? It is important that the leadership not take an overly dominant role. However, it is appropriate for the leadership to take a primary role in presenting new directions or changes. Senior staff might participate in small group sessions but must always remember they are group members, not leaders.

(continued)

Exhibit 5.4 (continued)

What is the best time to conduct a retreat and how frequently should they be held? The timing of a retreat is crucial only if the product that is being produced has some timeliness beyond the scope of the retreat. If the purpose of the retreat is to plan for the coming year, it should be timed so that the plan can be used to help build the budget for the new year. Long Beach managers recommend that a retreat be held prior to budget preparation and again in the summer to deal with other issues.

What products should result? Participants want tangible evidence that issues were dealt with in an effective way. The agency should prepare a memo describing key issues, suggestions, and planned actions arising from the retreat discussions.

— The meeting leader should have an agenda or at least a clear outline for the structure of the meeting.

— The meeting format should provide an opportunity for open-ended discussion and questions from staff. Meetings might also formally recognize the achievements of employees and other recent significant events.

— Each division should be given an opportunity to bring the rest of staff up-to-date on major accomplishments or items that are coming up that might affect or be of interest to other components of the department.

5.2(e) *Survey employees periodically*

The most sincere form of flattery is to listen. One method of listening more systematically to employees is to ask them to complete a questionnaire soliciting feedback on the organization. A manager who subsequently reviews and acts upon the compiled results has listened.

An agency annually or at some other interval might conduct an anonymous survey of all staff through a questionnaire about problems in the agency's working environment and obstacles to working productively. The questionnaire should contain both structured and open-ended questions that encourage staff to specify concerns and problems and to provide suggestions as to what improvement could be made to help them do their jobs better. A copy of the Knoxville questionnaire, distributed by the new CDA director after his arrival, is included in exhibit 5.5.

EXHIBIT 5.5

Staff Questionnaire

I.   In order for me to get to know you and the office, and most effectively prepare to do my job, I would like to get your honest input. Your answers are entirely voluntary, but would be very helpful. In addition, I will be meeting with each of you individually. Thanks.

(Signed by the Department Head)

A.   What do you like about Housing and Urban Affairs and your job?

B.   What do you dislike?

C.   What, if anything, would you change, add, delete, or modify?

II. Once a month, we will have a meeting of the entire staff. At that meeting, we will celebrate achievements, discuss any group concerns, and make sure that we have maximum communication between all the sections and personnel. We can also periodically have educational and informational programs and, if you like, covered dish luncheons.

A.   What type of educational or informational programs would you be most interested in (for instance, a program on the retirement system, a program on physical fitness, etc.)?

B.   Would you be interested in participating in a covered dish luncheon as part of the staff meeting?

If so, how often?   Once a month   ☐

Twice a month   ☐

Once a quarter ☐

Once a year   ☐

C.   What else would you like to see included as part of the staff meeting, or as a part of the activities of the Department?

Source: Knoxville, Tennessee, Department of Community Development, 1990.

5.2(f)   *Look for ways to enhance existing opportunities to communicate informally with staff*

Many opportunities exist during the work day to communicate and listen. At regular staff meetings, for example, vary the format periodically to include informal time for questions and comments at the *beginning*—before the meeting runs out of time. Rotate meeting time and location to accomodate staff who otherwise would have difficulty attending. This technique is especially applicable to staff who work in field offices and/or have nontraditional hours. In addition, a manager can create new opportunities for informal communication by varying the travel patterns the manager uses inside the office complex. This will cause the manager to "bump into" people located "off the beaten path."

ACTION 5.3

> *Encourage Genuine Staff Participation in Decision Making*
>
> (Primary sources: King County, Washington; Knoxville, Tennessee; Norman, Oklahoma; San Mateo County, California)

The key to buying into organizational goals is active involvement. The more that personnel are involved in the shaping of the organization's direction the more likely it is they will assume responsibility for getting there. In both King County and Knoxville, the mechanisms that the agencies used were not particularly remarkable, but the fact they actively included staff participation seemed to contribute to a successful outcome.

Knoxville   ➤   In Knoxville annual action plans are developed with considerable employee involvement. The specific targets are not set *for* the unit but *by* the staff in the unit. The ultimate responsibility for performance, however, still remains with the program and division managers and, in turn, with the agency head.

King County   ➤   King County requires that the performance of each employee be reviewed semi-annually, but the CDA has modified the process to require that the manager and employee *jointly* identify a specific development program for the employee for the next rating period. More on-the-job training or a chance to work on a task force or with a consultant or senior staff person may be identified to help the employee reach the development goal. This specific support from management enhances the employee's interest in improved performance. (See chapter 7 for discussion of performance tracking procedures and Appendix B for suggestions of performance indicators for which annual targets might be set.)

San Mateo County ➤ San Mateo County CDA professional staff also actively participate in the annual process to identify objectives relating to department goals. The CDA director also involved the staff in the development of the "Matrix Management System," an activity that increased staff buy-in.

Provide Incentives for Improved Performance
(Primary sources: Norman, Oklahoma; King County, Washington; Knoxville, Tennessee; Lower Merion Township, Pennsylvania)

ACTION 5.4

People like to be recognized for their efforts. The single most effective and simple form of recognition is to acknowledge an individual's contribution and say "thank you." This section discusses both informal and formal approaches to thanking employees, including appraisal processes that recognize employees' responsibilities and contributions to agency goals.

5.4(a) *Use a variety of mechanisms to recognize employee contributions*

"What gets recognized or rewarded, gets done." CDA directors can use a wide variety of mechanisms to recognize and reward employees performance. Exhibit 5.6 lists a number of such mechanisms. One note of caution: Spreading around rewards to too many staff will devalue all the awards. Most agencies, however, use recognition rewards too infrequently.

EXHIBIT 5.6

Mechanisms to Recognize and Reward Employee Performance

1. Write a letter of commendation to the employee

2. Compliment staff at meetings, both internal and external (such as at meetings of neighborhood organizations—and compliment appropriate neighborhood participants), for successes.

3. Provide written recognition as part of an employee's formal performance appraisal.

4. Give successful employees more responsibility.

5. Where government policy permits, consider financial bonuses or merit pay rates.

6. Provide training opportunities or chances to go to conferences and seminars.

7. Provide special and ad hoc assignments as a mark of distinction.

Norman ➤ In Norman, Oklahoma, the CDA director uses a wide variety of approaches. She takes one or more employees out to lunch or for refreshments after work to celebrate the start of a project, an individual or group accomplishment, or to show support during a particularly difficult period. She praises employees for their accomplishments and remembers to tell them that they are doing a good job, and she sends correspondence received from the public that commends employees to the city council and senior executive staff. In addition, she includes the names of the specific employees in staff reports made to elected officials concerning the performance of the department.

Award certificates are inexpensive but effective, especially if distributed by the manager at regular staff meetings or, if the achievement is of particular significance, by the chief elected or administrative officer. Awards might be given to teams of employees or individuals for completing a major project, completing the most projects during a particular period, making a recommendation that significantly increased productivity, being particularly helpful to clients or citizens, or recruiting the most clients during a particular period.

In Norman, the CDA has used award certificates to acknowledge employees' contributions to the agency (see exhibit 5.7).

King County ➤ King County instituted an informal award called the "Unsung Hero Award." This is intended to recognize in humorous fashion employees who are frequently overlooked and not in the public eye, such as word processors and statistical

EXHIBIT 5.7

Example of Recognition Certificate

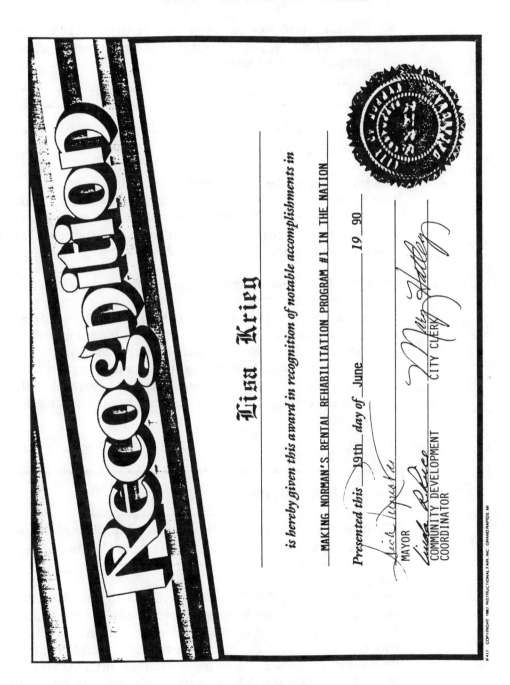

Source: Norman, Oklahoma, Planning Department, 1990.

specialists. The awards are made in an informal setting and are not announced in advance. One manager feels the element of surprise is important. The award ceremony includes an "Unsung Hero Certificate" prepared by the graphics department and gag gifts.

Knoxville ➤ Knoxville also provides awards and certificates, celebrates achievements at staff meetings, and posts positive letters and pictures on a "bragging wall."

5.4(b) *Increase employee responsibility to encourage good performance*

Employees should be discouraged from feeling they have to adhere strictly to their formal job descriptions. Instead, they should be delegated all the responsibility they are able and willing to handle. The broadening of responsibility will encourage staff creativity and concern for clients.

San Mateo County ➤ San Mateo County rehab team members are given sole responsibility for a territory and view their territory in rather possessive terms. For example, rehab specialists "market" directly to the residents in the team's neighborhood, taking additional application forms and going door-to-door to encourage people to apply for the program. This type of close identification with the client comes directly from the employees' feeling that they are responsible for the program.

ACTION 5.5

> ### Train Employees
>
> (Primary sources: Lower Merion Township, Pennsylvania; San Mateo County, California; Santa Ana, California)

Effective training imparts new skills to enhance employee performance and increase employee self-esteem and morale. Training can be used as a form of reward or recognition. It is also a way to communicate and listen to employees, and to contribute to team spirit. The most common form of training in CDAs is on-the-job training, but other forms include receiving coaching and mentoring from senior staff, and participating in task forces or formal programs conducted by agency personnel or outside consultants.

5.5(a) *Conduct periodic assessments of agency personnel training needs*

Such assessments will help identify what specific training is needed and for whom. This will better enable the CDA to plan how to use its scarce training resources. Such assessments should probably be done annually. Agencies can employ many approaches, including:

— Surveying managers for ideas on the training needed for their staff;

— Analyzing job descriptions and cataloging specific skills required;

— Surveying employees about their skills, job descriptions, what they feel is important to do their job well, whether staff skills (including their own) are adequate, and what training would help them do their job better.

5.5(b) *Provide cross training*

Where relevant, train staff to be able to take on a number of jobs, not just their own. This will enable them to fill in or take over for another employee who is absent or whose position is vacant. This also will enlarge the responsibility and capability of staff, potentially making their work more interesting.

Lower Merion Township ➢ As described under Action 5.1(b) in this chapter, Lower Merion Township provides informal cross training to its whole staff, including secretarial, on customer records, case problems, and the status of all projects. This training is accomplished by weekly briefings and on-the-job training.

San Mateo County ➢ Prior to forming rehab teams in San Mateo County, the agency had two specific types of rehab employees—loan officers and rehab specialists. The loan officer handled only loan-related aspects of rehab (i.e., applications and approval), while the rehab specialist handled only construction-related aspects. Position reclassification and cross training was conducted to ensure that rehab and loan specialists could perform certain aspects of each others' jobs. The new classification combined both rehab- and loan-related work. The result of cross training was that the new rehab specialist could make statements and commitments related to the loan *and* construction and not have to refer the client to someone else.

5.5(c)   *Measure training effectiveness*

A CDA should regularly ask persons attending training programs to provide feedback as to the quality, relevance, and helpfulness of the training they received. The supervisors of trainees should also be asked to assess whether staff skills, performance, or morale had been affected.

5.5(d)   *Train management and staff in new processes or procedures*

Ensuring that management is trained in new procedures and processes sends the message to staff that these changes are important and that management takes them seriously.

Santa Ana   ➤   In Santa Ana it was important to the acceptance of the quality team approach to have senior managers go through the same training as the employees. Upper management was not initially trained in the process, which led to problems when the quality teams made their recommendations to management. Team members felt they were not fully appreciated because management did not fully understand the quality team process.

San Mateo County   ➤   Similarly, San Mateo County found problems at the beginning of its implementation of Matrix Management due to lack of training of managers about what Matrix Management was. It became quite apparent that ongoing training for managers was needed to ensure the program's continued success.

Some Overall Concerns on Encouraging Employee Involvement

Involving employees in all aspects of their work is good management. Nevertheless, such involvement also presents problems that should be recognized and alleviated to the extent possible.

❐ Involvement requires managers to put in effort, time, and energy to work with employees. Meetings, retreats, and employee training and development require time of managers and staff. Managers should regard this time as part of their basic management responsibility. Nevertheless, organizations and managers under pressure will be tempted to cut corners in these activities, which will result in undercutting the otherwise positive effect of employee involvement.

❐ Meetings and retreats can become "old hat."

King County ➤ The King County, Washington CDA seeks new, hot management topics to debate at its management retreat to introduce fresh ideas and maintain group interest. Managers and staff need to be innovative to ensure these activities are interesting and productive.

❐ The encouragement of staff to provide ideas and to innovate by being involved should be supported by a corresponding willingness to implement good suggestions. If a CDA lacks the motivation, ability, or resources to implement new ideas, employees will soon become discouraged and refuse to participate. Building a climate where new ideas are valued, responsibility is delegated, and employees are trusted can encourage employees not only to generate but also to automatically implement actions under their control without having to seek permission from management.

❐ Employee involvement by no means solves all organizational problems. It does not guarantee a solid revenue base, and good performance and morale are not likely to be enough to win elected officials' full support of an agency's funding requests. In addition, some staff problems cannot be solved by employee participation efforts.

These techniques are not likely to be every manager's cup of tea. In spite of a sincere desire to implement some of these ideas, a manager's conflicting style or personality may pose a considerable obstacle to successful implementation. Thus, upper CDA management will need to "sell" the team approach to front-line and middle managers to increase its chances of success and, perhaps, provide training in the approach to its managers.

6

Contracting For Performance

ACTION 6.1 *Use a Systematic, Objective Process to Evaluate Proposals*

ACTION 6.2 *Provide Technical Assistance to Contractors*

 6.2(a) Provide workshops on CDA work-related matters

 6.2(b) Hold periodic group meetings with contractors to discuss contractor concerns and performance

ACTION 6.3 *Provide Special Assistance to Minority Contractors*

 6.3(a) Make special efforts to inform minority contractors of bidding opportunities

 6.3(b) Adjust operating procedures to help minority and small business contractors

 6.3(c) Make training available on various aspects of construction/rehabilitation

ACTION 6.4 *Use Performance or Incentive Contracting*

 6.4(a) Include specific performance targets as part of contracts

 6.4(b) Link payment to performance

 6.4(c) Use formal and informal awards to recognize high quality contractor performance

 6.4(d) Include quality of past work as a factor in renewing and awarding contracts

ACTION 6.5   *Monitor Contractors to Encourage Quality and Timely Performance*

6.5(a)   Include wording in the solicitation and the contract specifying the CDA's right to monitor contractor performance

6.5(b)   Make frequent site visits to monitor performance of contractors; consider past performance in determining frequency of visits

6.5(c)   Use a variety of procedures for monitoring

6.5(d)   Provide constructive feedback to contractors with significant problems

ACTION 6.6   *Evaluate Contractor Performance at the End of the Contract to Help with Future Choices of Contractors*

6.6(a)   Use various procedures, including obtaining input from recipients of services, to obtain information on contractor performance

Contracting for Performance

Most community development agencies (CDAs), both city and county, use contractors or subgrantees to help them deliver services. Counties use their municipalities as well as direct contractors. Cities and towns use housing rehab contractors and provide contracts or grants to non-profit organizations for a variety of services. The contractors and subgrantees represent the CDA. The way they perform affects the performance of the CDA.

A key concept of this chapter is that CDAs should not settle for work that only meets minimum quality standards. This chapter provides suggestions for encouraging a high level of performance by contractors.

For simplicity, throughout this chapter, we use the term contractor to encompass grantees as well. Almost all the suggestions presented apply to grants as well as contracts.

ACTION 6.1

> ## Use a Systematic, Objective Process to Evaluate Proposals
>
> (Primary sources: Cleveland, Ohio; Cuyahoga County, Ohio; Fairfax County, Virginia)

Developing a system to allocate community development funds as part of the competitive proposal process is an important aspect of contracting for performance. Such a system applies both to proposals submitted by private organizations and, in the case of county CDAs, to proposals submitted to them by their municipalities.

A key feature of a systematic, objective process is to select criteria to use in evaluating proposals. These criteria should be provided to potential proposers. Criteria to consider include:

— The extent to which the proposal serves target populations or areas;

— The extent to which the proposal addresses existing CDA priorities and objectives;

— The likely quality of the work proposed, based on past performance or personnel qualifications;

— Adherence to proposal requirements such as equal employment opportunity considerations; and

— Cost.

An objective rating system is needed to identify how each proposal "stacks up" against each of the criteria. Some CDAs apply relative weights to each of the criteria to reflect their relative importance.

Cuyahoga County ➤ Cuyahoga County uses a competitive project selection system for proposals submitted by its participating municipalities. Criteria include past performance of the applicant, number of low and moderate-income persons to be served, number of jobs to be created, and amount of money leveraged. Cuyahoga also includes criteria related to county goals, such as whether the municipality has a fair housing ordinance and an EEO-affirmative action plan, whether it has taken steps to encourage development of lower income housing, and whether the project includes participation of minority- or women-owned businesses.

CDAs should clearly explain the proposal process to proposers so that the process is perceived as fair and objective. Another important consideration is who will be involved in evaluating and rating the proposals. In general, CDA staff should be involved in this process, but representatives of particular sectors of the community, other government agency staff, or individuals with particular kinds of expertise can also participate. The raters selected should be fair and unbiased and viewed as such by others.

Cuyahoga County ➤ In Cuyahoga County scoring is done by the CDA manager and two other staff members, who challenge one another if there is significant disagreement among the scores. CDA staff visit each project site to assess the appropriateness of the project and to determine if other work needs to be done, for example, if the streets targeted for repair really need repair, or if a drainage problem needs to be addressed first. In cases such as the latter, CDA staff might recommend that the municipality modify its proposal. The perspectives from the site visits are factored into discretionary points that are awarded by a management team that includes the CDA manager, the two staff involved in the rating process, the heads of other interested county agencies, and a representative of the county administrator's office. This group brings to the process knowledge of the appropriateness of particular projects and the relative needs of different communities.

Cleveland   ➤ Cleveland uses a review board to assess proposals submitted for its technical assistance program. The 10-person review board includes a banker, a corporate representative, a foundation representative, two council members, and five CDA staff members. The external members of the board are chosen for their relevant experience. Each person on the board reviews and prepares comments on 6-7 proposals (out of approximately 30 submitted), using the evaluation forms prepared by staff as a guide for topics to address.

Selection of contractors for housing rehabilitation and similar work, however, is almost universally based solely on bid price. The lowest bidder gets the award. The justification for not considering the quality of the bidder's past performance is that rehabilitation work is sufficiently pre-specified so that as long as the work meets these standards, it will be satisfactory.

In our discussions with CDAs, some staff pointed out that the quality of work such as housing rehab, can differ considerably among contractors. They like the idea of including past performance quality as a criterion but do not know how it can be done. Currently, past performance can only be considered if a contractor's work has been sufficiently poor that the contractor is removed from a CDA's list of eligible bidders. The issue of excessive reliance on bid price to select contractors has also been raised in road construction and maintenance work, and some national experimentation has begun on alternatives.

However, until alternative criteria are developed, or CDAs experiment with the use of a request-for-proposal rather than request-for-bid process for housing rehab, the suggestions given in the remainder of this chapter will help encourage quality in request-for-bid situations.

ACTION 6.2

Provide Technical Assistance to Contractors
(Primary sources: Albany, New York; Cleveland, Ohio)

Technical assistance can help contractors do a better job for the CDA and the community. Such assistance can be in the form of formal training sessions such as workshops and seminars, and individualized technical assistance. CDA staff can provide the assistance or can contract with local colleges, non-profit organizations, such as a Small Business Development Corporation (SBDC), or for-profit consulting firms.

6.2 (a)   *Provide workshops on CDA work-related matters*

Non-profit service contractors in a number of cities and counties we visited expressed interest in receiving assistance on:

— Internal accounting procedures;

— Ways to better manage their own operations, including how to work better with staff, how to work under stress, and how to handle low staff compensation levels and high staff turnover;

— Staff training on working with clients, particularly difficult clients;

— Technical issues such as computerization of accounting systems, word processing, inventory control, and scheduling; and

— Fund raising.

A list of workshop topics for for-profit contractors, particularly small and minority contractors, is presented below under Action 6.3(c).

Providing workshops on particular CDA programs encourage better quality work, promote bidding, and increase the likelihood of successful bids by small and minority contractors, who are likely to be new to the business and in greater need of assistance.

Albany   ➤ One Albany workshop that was particularly helpful to minority contractors, although not intended solely for them, was an annual training session for paint contractors. CDA rehab staff members explained program requirements (e.g., what kind of paint to use, the meaning of specific terminology) and distributed handouts such as specifications, new regulations, and any forms required. The training was provided for painting contractors because this group has a high turnover and because it is a "foot in the door" business for new or small contractors, particularly minority businesses (because it requires low start-up costs and skills).

Workshops might also be provided on issues of special concern to the CDA.

Cuyahoga County ➤ Cuyahoga County provides half-day training sessions in fair housing issues for its participating municipalities. Participants in training sessions have included staff members from community development divisions, building commissioners, and elected officials. Sessions are held on topics such as landlord/tenant rights, new laws regarding handicapped discrimination, procedures for handling discrimination complaints, procedures for monitoring rental rehab/loans to ensure compliance with displacement and affirmative marketing policies, procedures for auditing real estate rental or sales practices, and financial counseling. Training sessions are presented by staff members of the organizations that provide these services for the county.

Contractors may also benefit from the kinds of training and technical assistance for small businesses discussed in chapter 3.

6.2(c) *Hold periodic group meetings with contractors to discuss contractor concerns and performance*

Such meetings should be held at least once a year, more often if contractors are not performing satisfactorily. The findings from the CDA's contract monitoring and evaluating efforts (see Actions 6.5 and 6.6) should be discussed at these meetings, and good performance should be commended.

Group meetings should focus on new policies and regulations, and on identifying concerns held by the contractors and how these might be alleviated. Contractors who have not bid on work or who did bid but did not receive contracts should also be invited, since one purpose of these meetings is to encourage interest in, and bidding on, CDA work.

Cleveland ➤ Cleveland holds such meetings for all its rehab contractors twice a year. At one meeting, contractors reported a problem in payments not being processed promptly. The department was able to speed up the process. At another meeting, contractors complained that they were having problems with aluminum siding being stolen from worksites (because aluminum could be sold for recycling). The department subsequently allowed the substitution of vinyl siding, which was not as readily saleable.

ACTION 6.3

Provide Special Assistance to Minority Contractors

(Primary sources: Albany, New York; Cleveland, Ohio; Lower Merion Township, Pennsylvania)

Technical assistance is especially important to minority-owned contractors, whose staff are likely to be small or relatively inexperienced. Such assistance can encourage growth of minority business and the jobs associated with it and ultimately increase the number of contractors available to deliver CDA services.

6.3(a)

Make special efforts to inform minority contractors of bidding opportunities

The following suggestions primarily apply to projects where bidding is held, such as housing rehabilitation. These steps are particularly relevant if the CDA is not receiving enough bids from minority contractors.

❑ If there is a minority contractors' association, make sure it is informed about the potential opportunities for its members.

❑ Obtain directories of minority business enterprises and use the directories to notify them of the CDA's program. Write letters and/or make telephone calls to each appropriate business, encouraging them to get on the CDA's list of bidders. Address letters to the company owner rather than sending a form letter. (Minority contractors told us this would make the letter considerably more appealing.)

❑ Advertise in local newspapers targeted to minorities, emphasizing that minority business contractors are welcome (see exhibit 6.1).

❑ Ask building material suppliers located in or near minority areas to post CDA announcements encouraging contractors to contact the CDA for information on future work.

❑ Develop a list of minority contractors and businesses to target when sending out notices on competitions. Make the list available to general contractors seeking minority

EXHIBIT 6.1

Sample Advertisement for Contractors

Paint Contractors

The Albany Community
Development Agency needs
you to perform $200,000 of
painting starting in the spring of 1989.

Building Contractors

The Agency also needs qualified
contractors to participate in its
Housing Rehabilitation program.

New expanded projects
**Streamlined payment
procedures**
All Contractors welcome!

Contact:
Spiro Takes
Rehabilitation Director
Albany Community Development Agency
155 Washington Ave.
Albany, N.Y. 12210
434-5259

Source: Albany, New York, Department of Housing and Community Development, 1989.

subcontractors. Have staff recruit minority businesses they come into contact with when they participate in small- or minority business programs or other minority-focused events.

Albany ➤ Albany's minority-affairs officer tries to attract new firms for its list of contractors by asking minority business enterprise personnel at worksites to refer others for inclusion in the list, by attending community events in the minority community to informally recruit MBEs at these events, and by providing a training workshop on how to obtain minority business certification.

❐ Check the procedures used to notify contractors about requests-for-proposals to ensure that they do not unintentionally exclude or discourage minority firms. For example, procedures should discourage staff from falling into the routine of informally notifying only a small group of established contractors.

❐ To the extent this can legally be done, make special arrangements to include at least one minority contractor among those invited to bid on each job. This arrangement might be used when a minority contractor first becomes certified by the agency, to help make the firm more viable and competitive.

6.3(b) *Adjust operating procedures to help minority and small business contractors*

Minority contractors identified the following actions needed by the CDA to enable them to participate.

❐ Pay contractor bills quickly to reduce cash flow problems. Three weeks after an invoice is received is reasonable. Permit more frequent billing.

Lower Merion Township ➤ Lower Merion Township switched from monthly to biweekly payments to rehab contractors. It also switched from a procedure in which nonprofit organizations were responsible for paying contractors to a process in which the Township paid them after gaining the nonprofit organization's approval. These steps greatly expedited payments and reduced complaints from contractors.

❏ Keep terminology on job specification clear and simple, and keep the paperwork as brief as possible.

❏ Provide potential rehab contractors with the name, home and daytime telephone numbers, and address of the client whose home is to be rehabilitated, so the contractor does not waste time locating the client for an appointment to look at the home in order to make a cost estimate for its bid to the CDA.

❏ Attempt to help with, or alleviate, bonding costs such as bid and performance bonds. Minority and other small business contractors are likely to have special problems getting these. At a minimum, provide technical assistance to help businesses find the least expensive bonding organizations.

❏ Provide ample bidding opportunities for minority contractors. For CDAs that limit bid invitations on individual jobs to a small number of firms, the CDA needs a fair system for choosing which to invite to bid on each project. This might be done randomly or by rotation. CDAs need to ensure that race/ethnicity is not a reason for selecting those invited to bid. In cases where agencies permit the owner to select a contractor other than the lowest bidder (if the owner pays the difference), the CDA needs to ensure that race/ethnicity is not the reason for rejecting the lowest bidder.

❏ Provide constructive feedback to minority contractors having problems meeting contractual obligations. Assist minority businesses to ensure that their work meets quality standards. Make deficiencies clear to contractors and suggest ways to improve their work.

❏ Encourage or assist potential minority contractors to apply for state or local small business loans, including those loans oriented toward minority businesses.

6.3(c)   *Make training available on various aspects of construction/rehabilitation*

Minority businesses expressed considerable interest in obtaining training and technical assistance on (1) obtaining financing, (2) cost estimating, (3) accounting with particular attention to taxes, payroll, and depreciation of capital costs, (4) insurance, and (5) bonding.

Ask one or more leading construction companies in the community to provide volunteers to develop and teach such a course. Use a committee or task force consisting of representatives from construction firms, CDA rehab staff, and minority contractors to determine course content.

Cleveland ➤ For about 20 years, a major construction company in Cleveland has offered an annual 10-week construction management training seminar in cooperation with Cleveland's Minority Business Development Center. The Center provides advertising, refers people to it, and handles registration. Approximately 40-45 "students" attend each year. The seminar consists of two 2-hour classes per week on weekday evenings and is held at a local university. It is primarily taught by construction company staff, with some sessions taught by CPAs, lawyers, or insurance personnel. A fee of $185 is charged to participants to cover expenses, including the course "text," a large looseleaf folder of materials designed for the course. Topics covered include: (1) Contracts, (2) Marketing, (3) You and Your General Contractor, (4) Pre-Job/Pre-Start Planning and Engineering, (5) Daily Operations and Control, (6) Business Plans and Organization, (7) Estimating Costs, (8) Purchasing Procedures, (9) Field Accounting/Cost Reports, (10) Financial Statements, (11) Accounting and Bookkeeping, and (12) Insurance and Bonding.

ACTION 6.4

> ## Use Performance or Incentive Contracting
>
> (Primary sources: Albany, New York; Charlotte, North Carolina; Cuyahoga County, Ohio; Hartford, Connecticut; Fairfax County, Virginia)

By specifying objectives to be met and subsequently monitoring performance, CDAs can encourage contractors to perform at a high level and make them more accountable for service quantity, quality, and timeliness. The agency can also reward effective contractors by renewing contracts, expanding the scope of existing contracts, and considering past performance of those proposing or bidding for new work.

Performance contracting requires writing performance requirements into contracts. This places the CDA in a stronger position to encourage quality performance and withhold payments if performance requirements are not met.

"Incentive contracting" goes further. Here the contract specifies rewards for achieving specific performance targets, or penalties for not achieving them. These rewards and penalties are usually monetary. This approach provides even greater incentives to for-profit contractors, but has also been used for non-profit service organizations. It is best used when the extent of achievement of important objectives is accurately measurable. One example is contracts whose payments are based on the number of eligible clients placed in jobs. The more clients placed in jobs by the contractor, the more the contractor gets paid.

Performance contracting has considerable application to CDAs; incentive contracting has less because of its added complications. Examples of both forms of contracting are described below.

6.4(a) *Include specific performance targets as part of contracts*

Request for proposals (RFPs) should ask potential contractors or grantees to express objectives in quantifiable terms, identifying specific performance indicators. Performance targets should typically include the number of clients to be served and *indicators of service quality* wherever possible. Targets should be specified for each reporting period as well as for the full contract period—to permit the CDA to track actual performance against targets. Appendix B contains examples of such indicators.

For services being provided directly to clients by the contractors, such as training, counseling, transportation, and housing rehabilitation, consider including performance targets tied to feedback on client satisfaction. This might be done, for example, by surveying all or a sample of past and current clients. An actual target level of client satisfaction might be included in the contract. Even if this is not done, however, the RFP and contract should make it clear that the contractor will be monitored and evaluated in part on service quality and customer satisfaction and that the contractor is expected to respond to any problems. Procedures for obtaining information on service quality are described under Actions 6.5 and 6.6.

As necessary, the agency should work with the contractor to develop appropriate and meaningful performance targets.

Fairfax County ➤ The Fairfax County Department of Community Action, for its contracts to help lower income families find housing, requires contractors to provide data monthly on the following to help it assess contract (and program) effectiveness: (1) number of persons provided assistance in remaining in present home; (2) number of persons assisted in finding permanent housing; (3) number of persons placed in permanent housing; (4) number of evictions prevented for those that had received "pay or quit" notices; (5) number of utility cutoffs prevented; and (6) number of persons placed in temporary housing (an "intermediate outcome" indicator).

Charlotte ➤ Charlotte uses a Contracting-by-Objectives form of performance contracting for its service providers. Service contracts must include a section detailing the objectives to be achieved. Exhibit 6.2 presents an example of performance targets written into a contract for its home management and assistance program. Charlotte encourages contractors to set the objectives themselves, but staff negotiate with contractors if the department feels the objectives are too low. More extensive negotiations are usually needed for new contractors who lack experience in setting effective objectives.

Hartford ➤ Hartford's contracts specify measurable objectives. For example, a contract for food to the homeless included the goals of serving 6,000 additional meals to the homeless in the Hartford area, and enhancing the quality of meals served through the purchase of fresh food. The objectives were to serve an additional 6,000 meals and purchase and serve an additional $4,200 of fresh food and produce above the previous year's baseline.

➤ Hartford's "Hispanic Employability, Learning and Placement Project" contract included targets for the number of individuals: recruited and tested, enrolled in the basic education program, completing the basic education course, achieving minimum scores of 60 on the English post-test and increasing their scores by at least 10 points over the pre-test, obtaining minimum scores of 60 on the mathematics post-test and increasing their scores by at least 10 points over the pre-test, placed in permanent full-time jobs, remaining in such jobs 90 days after placement, and also in such jobs 6 months after placement.

But don't just insert performance requirements into contracts— track the contractor's actual performance against these targets and provide appropriate feedback. When significant deficiencies appear, discuss those with the contractor. Attempt to identify the reasons for deficiencies and encourage the contractor to correct them.

EXHIBIT 6.2

Example of Contract Wording on Objectives

Objectives for Home Management and Improvement Contracts

1. *Improve* the conditions of *owner* and *tenant occupied homes*, the financial stability and home management skills of not less than 1,800 City of Charlotte low and moderate income families by providing professional individual or group counseling and/or Consumer Education in one or more of the service areas described under *general counseling and consumer education services*.

2. *Work* with not less than 40 persons who are Public Housing residents or on the Public Housing waiting list to help facilitate eligibility for a second mortgage loan for home-ownership. This is intended to develop a pool of persons who will be able to take advantage of homeownership opportunities.

3. *Provide* pre-purchase and post-occupancy counseling to selected residents of prospective City-assisted housing projects by providing not less than three (3) one-hour personal counseling sessions of each type with the pre-purchase sessions occurring prior to occupancy.

4. *Provide* mortgage default counseling to delinquent housing rehabilitation borrowers referred by the Community Development Department by taking the appropriate actions to bring current delinquent loans in line, as outlined in attachment B.

5. *Prevent* homeowner mortgage foreclosures for 75% of the homeowners assisted with mortgage delinquencies, excluding the delinquent housing rehabilitation borrowers.

6. *Prevent* eviction for not less than 65% of the tenants assisted for rental delinquency.

7. *Prevent* eviction for not less than 65% of the tenants assisted for rental property abuse referral from Realtors.

8 *Provide* not less than twelve (12) sessions of *consumer education classes* during the contract period, concentrating in low to moderate City of Charlotte Neighborhoods, focusing primarily on Household Budgeting.

9 *Initiate* service to referral with emergency type problems within five (5) work days.

Source: Charlotte, North Carolina, Community Development Department, 1990.

6.4(b) *Link payment to performance*

If contractors fail to meet contract performance levels, contracts should permit penalties to be instituted. Penalties can take the form of (a) withholding payments because of incomplete work, (b) reducing the size of the contract, or (c) terminating the contract because of poor performance. As noted earlier, performance can also be linked to payments through the amount and quality of the final product delivered. Some contracts might be written so that contractors are paid on a "per-unit" basis. Contracts can also include monetary bonus clauses such as bonuses if the contractor completes the specified work before the target date or considerably exceeds the client satisfaction levels targeted by the contract.

No matter what type of performance link is used, incentives and penalties should be clearly stated in the contract.

Contracts involving monetary incentives, especially penalty provisions, have special problems. Contractors will often not take penalties lying down. They will battle the agency, and perhaps take legal action. Therefore, penalty provisions should be very carefully considered before being included into contracts to ensure that the penalty criteria can be measured objectively and validly.

Bonus clauses and unit-price contracts that establish positive incentives can encourage performance. These incentives for added quantity or quicker service delivery should be rewarded only if the *quality* of the product is appropriate. These monetary incentives should only be used if the agency can adequately measure quality and can do so in a way that the contractor accepts.

Albany ➢ Albany has contracted with Neighborhood Improvement Corporations (NIC) to recruit and screen homeowners for CDA rehab programs. The system had been in place for over 10 years, but as the result of performance standards not being used and the NICs referring fewer and fewer customers for rehab projects, HUD cut back on the CDA's funding in the mid-1980s. In response, the new director of the CDA instituted an incentive contracting system, under which NICs have met their performance targets: the CDA reports a 300 percent increase in residential rehab cases after moving to incentive contracting. Under the new system, the NICs are required to submit an agreed on number of qualified applications to the CDA per contract year. If they have not achieved half of that target at their six-month progress review, their monthly payments for the remainder of the year are reduced by a specific amount for each application short of the target. If the NIC makes up the shortage in the final six months, the amounts deducted are returned to the NIC. At the end of the second half of the contract, the NIC's progress in meeting its objectives is again reviewed. If the NIC has failed to reach its target for the year, a penalty of $1,000 is deducted from the final payment for each application submitted less than the target. If the NIC has submitted applications in excess of its target, the number of referrals for the upcoming year is reduced by the amount exceeded (up to a maximum of three credits). In the event that the NIC did not obtain two-thirds of the total number of required referrals, the NIC is not eligible for funding in the upcoming contract year.

Hartford ➤ Hartford sometimes uses a "fee for services rendered" payment structure. Sub-grantees who serve meals to the homeless are reimbursed on a price-per-meal served basis, and training and employment contractors are paid per student achieving the various performance targets specified in the contract, e.g., so many dollars per "student placed in permanent full-time employment and retained for at least 90 days."

6.4(c) *Use formal and informal awards to recognize high quality contractor performance*

Non-monetary awards such as certificates, plaques, and recognition events can also be used to motivate contractors to perform well. These do not require as strict a set of criteria and performance measurements as do monetary incentives. Non-monetary awards can be used for sub-grantees and rehab contractors alike. Annual recognition awards for each type of work can provide encouragement (at low cost) to for-profit and non-profit, public and private contractors and grantees.

Albany ➤ Albany holds an annual "contractors' breakfast" at which the CDA awards plaques to the general contractor and painting contractor with the highest ratings average. Three runner-up plaques are provided to contractors with scores very close to the "winners."

Cuyahoga County ➤ Cuyahoga County presents several different awards to participating municipalities that received grant funds in the prior year. Plaques or certificates are presented in different categories such as: certificate for well-administered projects, best overall project award, fair housing award, and certificate for passing a fair housing ordinance. The awards are distributed during a luncheon ceremony held as part of the CDA's annual, day-long training session on the proposal process.

For these awards to be effective in encouraging contractors to excel in their work, the contractors have to know about them in advance. Thus, the CDA needs to publicize them widely at the beginning of each year. The awards ceremony for the past year can be used to kick off publicity for the next year's awards.

How to evaluate contractors in order to objectively determine those deserving rewards is described under Action 6.6.

6.4(d)   *Include quality of past work as a factor in renewing and awarding contracts*

CDAs can and do drop contractors after repeated quality or timeliness problems. Performance on past work for the government should be included, wherever possible, as an explicit evaluation criterion when contracts come up for renewal. Using "requests for proposals" rather than "requests-for-bids" (which require that the lower bidder gets the contract) permits CDAs to consider factors other than cost when awarding contracts.

As discussed earlier under Action 6.1 pertaining to criteria to include in CDA solicitations, the situation differs for housing rehabilitation. While contractors chronically exhibiting problems can be removed from the CDA's list of bidders, those remaining on the list can differ significantly in the quality of their work and timeliness. Housing rehab "requests-for-bids" solicitations normally have to be awarded to the lowest bidder. Requests-for-proposal procedures might be used for housing rehab, but would break with tradition and pose legal questions. If the additional criterion of past performance can be added to the contracting process, such as by giving a weight to both past performance and price, the method of determining the past performance rating will have to be strictly specified to be fair to all those submitting proposals.

Charlotte   ➤ Charlotte evaluates contractor performance after nine months. If contractors have not meet their objectives, the department can use this as a basis for not renewing the contract.

Albany   ➤ Albany uses a "performance and work history report" to assess rehab contractor performance. That information is used for decisions about the contractor's eligibility for future work. If the contractor has received a poor rating on more than one project, the rehab director will call the contractor in to discuss the problem and offer advice. For example, if the contractor is having difficulty with subcontractors or having difficulty finding subcontractors, the rehab director refers the contractor to other subcontractors. Contractors can be dropped from the CDA's list for poor ratings.

ACTION 6.5

Monitor Contractors to Encourage Quality and Timely Performance

(Primary sources: Charlotte, North Carolina; Cleveland, Ohio; Fairfax County, Virginia; Norman, Oklahoma; Rock Island, Illinois; San Mateo County, California)

It is vital that CDAs monitor work performed by sub-grantees and contractors. Most do, one way or another. Here we provide suggestions for strengthening that process to encourage quality performance.

The term "monitoring" refers to the process of obtaining regular feedback on whether work on on-going contracts is proceeding as it should. The information sought should cover both an assessment of the way the service is being delivered and the quality of that delivery. Feedback from monitoring provides early warning of problems so that necessary improvements can be made. Monitoring should be done at regular intervals throughout the contract period, at least on a quarterly basis. Monitoring information can also be used to assess overall contractor performance for use in renewal and future contracting decisions.

"Evaluation" refers to a more in-depth, less frequent examination as to how the contractor has performed, particularly in relation to the contract's objectives. Evaluation should usually be performed near or at the end of the term of a contract. Below are actions needed to monitor contractors properly. Action 6.6 spells out suggestions for evaluating contractors.

6.5(a) *Include wording in the solicitation and the contract specifying the CDA's right to monitor contractor performance*

Potential contractors should be explicitly alerted in the solicitation and in the contract that the agency expects to monitor (and evaluate) the results and performance of the contractor. The contract should also require the contractor to correct any deficiencies identified. An example of contract wording addressing these requirements is shown in exhibit 6.3.

The contractor should be made contractually responsible for providing the necessary information to the CDA for review, including regular reports on progress toward meeting contract goals and objectives. The contractor should also be notified that the agency has a right to interview clients to help assess performance.

EXHIBIT 6.3

Example of Contract Wording on Monitoring and Evaluation

The City reserves the right to monitor the manner, means, and details of the delivery of services by the Contractor, as well as to evaluate the goals to be accomplished. The Contractor agrees to comply with evaluation and information requirements, including but not limited to: site visits, program or fiscal audits, and periodic and annual reports. The Contractor shall comply fully with all recommendations and requirements of the City resulting from such evaluations and audits which are deemed by the City to be consistent with the provision of services under the contract.

The Contractor shall correct any deficiencies identified by the City in a reasonable period of time to be determined by the City.

Failure to comply with the recommendations of the City in the provision of services herein described shall be considered a violation of this Agreement and sufficient reason for termination of same.

Source: Hartford, Connecticut, Boilerplate for CDBG Contract for Professional Services, 1990.

6.5(b)   *Make frequent site visits to monitor performance of contractors; consider past performance in determining frequency of visits*

The frequency of monitoring visits will depend on the amount of staff available relative to the number, size, and complexity of projects being monitored. Visits on most contracts should probably be done at least quarterly and probably no more than monthly unless major problems have been found in prior visits. For work such as housing rehab, some CDAs undertake daily site visits.

Consider establishing a classification scheme that assigns different frequencies of visits to contractors based on their past performance. (Other factors should also be considered in determining frequency, such as complexity, size, and importance of project.) Contractors and sub-grantees whose past performance indicates the presence of or potential for problems should be monitored more frequently.

The frequency of visits should be based on how well the contractor has been doing in meeting contract objectives or performance criteria.

Cleveland   ➤   Cleveland uses the following levels in its classification scheme:

— If service provider is not providing adequate service or has poor documentation, *monitor as often as needed* to improve the service level;

— If performance is not consistently up to the expected level set forth in the contract, *monitor monthly*;

— If performance consistently meets and sometimes slightly exceeds the expected level, *monitor quarterly*;

— If performance is consistently far above expectations, *monitor twice a year*.

Exhibit 6.4 provides some additional suggestions for site monitoring visits.

6.5(c)   *Use a variety of procedures for monitoring*

Monitoring activities can be informal or formal. CDAs should conduct regular formal monitoring and use informal monitoring as a supplement. Formal monitoring involves written submission and compilation of information for use in some "official" way, such as in a monitor's report to CDA officials or the city or county council. Formal monitoring should include written feedback to contractors on the findings.

For informal monitoring, the information obtained is not compiled or used in an official way. For example, notes may be taken and inserted in a contractor's file, but a written report is not submitted. When an important problem is discovered through informal monitoring, staff may then need to take more formal action to correct the problem.

The monitoring effort should seek information on service quality as well as on how providers are doing their work. One way is to seek feedback from customers. This should encourage contractors to focus on responsiveness to customers as an explicit part of their activities. Appendix B provides an illustrative list of performance indicators for a number of CDA programs. These are candidates for monitoring and for inclusion in the contracts themselves.

The following are some examples of CDA monitoring practices:

Rock Island
San Mateo County
Norman

➤ Rehab staff in Rock Island and San Mateo County make weekly unscheduled site visits to housing rehab projects. Housing rehab specialists in Norman visit each rehab project daily. All three agencies make it a point to talk to the homeowner and ask if there are any problems. If the client reports problems, these are brought to the attention of the contractor. Staff also check on the materials, quality of work, and code requirements.

EXHIBIT 6.4

Suggestions to Enhance the Effectiveness of Formal Monitoring Visits

1. Bring a copy of the work specifications. Check items off as done or partially done and mark items that should be checked in future visits. For housing rehab projects and the like, look at materials present on the project site to be sure they are as specified. (If not, this may indicate that the contractor is not reading the specs.) Identify any problems in materials or work, including materials used before installation.

2. Talk with the contractor. Ask how things are going, if there are any problems, and whether change orders are needed or anticipated, whether customers are being cooperative.

3. Talk with customers of the contractor. Ask if things are going well and if they have any problems. This can be done by phone if necessary. For those housing rehab items where the customer has a choice to make, also make inquiries along the lines of "have you selected your paint colors yet?" to ensure that the contractor is giving the customer the opportunity to choose. If this is a service contract with many customers, speak with a small sample. If problems are indicated by those sampled, sample more customers to confirm the problems.

4. Use a rating form to keep track of the items to be examined during each visit and to document the findings. Rate the contractor's progress related to timeliness; quality of work done; and, for service contracts/grants, the extent to which the sub-grantee is using sound accounting, record-keeping, and staffing practices. Describe in writing specific problems found during the monitoring visit.

5. When problems are found, notify the contractor in writing, and work with him to get them corrected. Written notice will also provide documentation if legal action is subsequently taken by any party.

6. Shortly after the visit, debrief the contractor orally. Some prefer to do this at the end of the visit before leaving the site.

7. Make at least some unannounced visits. This will provide some assurance that contractors are performing as desired, not just doing so when expecting inspectors.

8. Periodically rotate inspectors to avoid their becoming overly friendly with contractors/grantees, thus reducing their objectivity. This problem is more likely to occur with multi-year work or where the same contractors regularly do work for the agency. Rotation on short (one year or less) contracts is probably not desirable because it involves loss of the inspector's familiarity with the project.

Fairfax County ➤ The Fairfax County Department of Community Action, for its housing counseling and placement service contracts, during each quarterly visit telephones 10 to 20 clients served by each housing counselor. The brief interview asks if they received services, what the results were (e.g., did they get permanent housing), whether they were satisfied with the service, and whether they have any complaints (and, if so, what they are).

Cleveland ➤ Cleveland conducts periodic site visits to monitor service providers. During these visits, staff conduct in-person interviews with two to three clients present to determine: activities the client participated in, how the client became aware of the program, how well the staff treated the client, how client rated the program, and if the client had suggestions for improving the service or programs.

Fairfax County ➤ Fairfax County has a standardized form called a "Contractual, Programmatic and Financial Review Guide." It is filled out by the monitor after a site visit, and is used to indicate whether or not the monitor has found the contractor to be in conformance with each regulation and each section of the contract, and to provide comments where appropriate. The inspection includes a review of the contractor's progress in relation to goals and objectives in the contract.

More details on ways to collect monitoring data, especially on service quality, are outlined under Action 6.6.

To ensure objectivity, the agency itself may prefer to gather data directly on service quality, especially customer-feedback data. However, for contracts serving many people, the CDA can require the contractors themselves to obtain feedback from their customers. This saves the CDA time and effort and has the further advantage of sensitizing the contractor to customer needs. Disadvantages of this approach are discussed under Action 6.6(a).

Charlotte ➤ In Charlotte, data on meeting contract objectives is generally collected by the service provider and forwarded to the CDA for review. The department ensures reliability of the data by requiring monthly reports from the contractor, staff quarterly site visits during which data collection procedures and records are reviewed, and a nine-month in-depth evaluation by agency staff. If needed, technical assistance is given to the contractor, and a re-examination of the objectives can take place.

Hartford ➤ Hartford requires service contractors to complete a progress form with each bill the contractor sends to the CDA. The form shows achievements to date on each performance target in the contract, and has space to explain any deviation from planned progress. Exhibit 6.5 is an example of the contractor reporting form.

6.5(d) *Provide constructive feedback to contractors with significant problems*

CDA staff should quickly follow up on significant problems identified in monitoring inspections by providing constructive feedback and offering assistance to the contractor where appropriate. If the contractor continues to have problems, the CDA needs to take more drastic action such as terminating the current contract and suspending the contractor from future bidding.

Charlotte ➤ In Charlotte, the monitor found problems with the financial reports of a contractor because the contractor's bookkeeper was not able to keep up with the financial program paperwork. The monitor arranged for financial accounting training using personal computers through a course offered by the city's Management Information System Department. This enabled the contractor to computerize data, improving the accounting process.

ACTION 6.6

Evaluate Contractor Performance at the End of the Contract to Help with Future Choices of Contractors

(Primary sources: Albany, New York; Charlotte, North Carolina; Fairfax County, Virginia; Rock Island, Illinois)

The performance of the contractor should be evaluated near or after the end of the contract period. As noted under Action 6.5(a), wording giving the CDA access to information needed to conduct an evaluation should be included in contracts. Such information will better enable the CDA to make future decisions regarding renewals and new contract awards.

EXHIBIT 6.5

Sample Contract Reporting Form

CDBG WORKPLAN AND REPORT SERVICES

Project Name: Hispanic Employability, Learning and
Placement Project

Address: Hartford, Conn

Contact Person:
Project Director:

Contract Period:

Goal(s): A. To increase participants' competencies in English and Math and to enhance their employability.

B. To assist 20 individuals to secure permanent full-time employment.

Performance Measures		1990						1991						Total
		July	Aug.	Sept.	Oct.	Nov.	Dec.	Jan.	Feb.	Mar.	April	May	June	
1. # Individuals recruited and tested	Target	15						15						30
	Actual	12												
2. Cycle I – Individuals enrolled in basic education	Target	12												12
	Actual													
3. Cycle I – Individuals completing basic education	Target						12							12
	Actual													
4. Cycle II – Individuals enrolled in basic education	Target							12						12
	Actual													
5. Cycle II – Individuals completing basic education	Target								12					12
	Actual													
6. Ref. #4, Goals & Objectives	Target						10		10					20
	Actual													
7. Ref. #5, Goals & Objectives	Target						10		10					20
	Actual													
8. # individuals placed in perm/FT job	Target										10		10	20
	Actual													
9. # individuals in such jobs 90 days after placement	Target						10				10			(see next page)
	Actual													
10. # individuals in such jobs 6 mos. after placement	Target	10												20
	Actual													

Source: Hartford, Connecticut, Office of Community Development and Planning, 1990, extract from CDBG Reporting Form.

As a standard practice, evaluations should be formal in nature with a final report issued to appropriate officials. Furthermore, as discussed in chapter 7, information from these evaluations can be used by the CDA in evaluating the overall performance of specific programs. These evaluations can also be used as the basis for monetary and non-monetary recognition of good performance, as discussed under Action 6.4.

Evaluations should include contractor's performance on both the quantitative requirements and quality of that work, including such elements as helpfulness to clients, timeliness, and meeting schedules.

A copy of the contractor performance report should be entered into a formal file kept on each contractor. Such a file should also contain monitoring information on that contractor. This file should be made available for future use when the CDA or any other government agency is considering future proposals by that contractor. The review of proposals from contractors should include a formal step to review past performance by the contractors (see Action 6.1). This procedure should be announced in requests for proposals or solicitations as encouragement to provide quality performance on all contracts.

Fairfax County ➤ Fairfax County conducts an annual combined evaluation and monitoring inspection. It also has conducted a special evaluation process that includes sending a questionnaire to service contractors asking the contractor to list its achievements against each performance goal specified in the contract. CDA staff complete another section of that form, a section that summarizes: achievement for each goal, monitoring findings, deficiencies, financial information, and other concerns—for each program year. Finally, the form asks for the staff's recommendations regarding performance and future funding.

Charlotte ➤ Charlotte conducts an evaluation of service contractors' performance in the ninth month of the contract. If a contractor has not met an objective specified in the contract, the evaluators report the reasons and identify actions the contractor or the agency needs to take to correct the problem. If the evaluation indicates that performance has not been satisfactory, the current contract can be put on hold until the problem is corrected, or final payment can be withheld as an incentive for the contractor to meet the objectives. An example of the objectives included in contracts and against which they are subsequently monitored and evaluated was shown in exhibit 6.2.

For services such as housing rehabilitation, where CDA awards are generally based on bid price alone, the CDA is more limited in how it can use evaluation information. However, keeping evaluation information in contractors' files will enable the CDA to more easily assess whether the performance of particular contractors has been sufficiently poor to warrant their being taken off the eligible list of bidders. This documentation may be needed if any legal action is brought by the contractor.

Albany ➤ In Albany the rehab specialist assigned to each project completes a performance and work history report, rating on a scale of 1 to 10 the contractor's work on the project in terms of quality of contractor work, quality of subcontractor work, coordination with subcontractors, timeliness of completion, and contractor's ability to communicate with homeowner. The ratings are based on the rehab specialist's judgment. Although the homeowner is not consulted in preparing these ratings, the rehab specialist is in contact with the homeowner during the course of the project and asks if there were any problems with the contractor at the time the homeowner signs off on the project. The ratings for the five items are added. Scores in the 1-31 range are considered unsatisfactory; 32-43, average; 44-50, above average.

The CDA should contact contractors after they have received one or more deficient evaluations, and when appropriate, put contractors on notice that they will be dropped from the bidder list if this occurs again. At the same time, however, the CDA should offer to explore with the contractor the reasons for its poor performance ratings and be ready to provide suggestions as to how to improve its rating in the future. This may lead to improved contractor performance.

Some service contracts can last for multiple years with annual renewal options. In such cases, the CDA should undertake evaluations prior to renewal decisions.

Evaluations held before the end of the contract year have the disadvantage of missing possible poor performance in the final months of the contract. To alleviate this problem, the CDA can make the renewal conditional on satisfactory completion of the contract. In such cases, the CDA could undertake a supplemental evaluation at the end of the 12-month period. Renewal contracts can also include clauses calling for postponing payments until problems from the previous contract have been corrected. This may be a more politically palatable step than having to suspend a contract that has been recently approved by local elected officials.

6.6(a) *Use various procedures, including obtaining input from recipients of services, to obtain information on contractor performance*

Use any or all of these three basic data sources to obtain evaluation (and monitoring) information:

— agency and contractor records;

— observations by trained observers; and

— surveys of customers of the contractor.

Appendix B contains an illustrative list of performance indicators that a CDA might use for various programs, and indicates which of the above sources are appropriate for each indicator.

Many CDAs already receive feedback from clients of housing rehabilitation programs. However, such feedback is often verbal and informal. For the purpose of systematic evaluation, a more formal approach should be used, such as a questionnaire or form for homeowners to fill out. Informal, undocumented responses from clients will generally not provide adequate tracking of contractor performance over time. Also, informal, memory-driven evidence is much less likely to hold up in court if legal action is taken as a result of a contractor's poor performance. The existence of formal documentation can discourage disgruntled contractors from taking legal action.

The CDA should attempt to obtain responses from a high percentage of all the contractor's clients or of a representative sample so the findings give an accurate picture of the contractor's performance.

Charlotte ➢ In Charlotte, at the close of each rehabilitation job, a questionnaire is given to the homeowner with a self-addressed stamped envelope. Homeowners are asked to mail the form back with their responses. The questionnaire is short (one page, nine questions), and includes such questions as Were you pleased with the rehabilitation work? Were city staff helpful? Were city staff courteous? Were you satisfied with the time it took to process your loan/grant application and to complete the repairs to your house? Were there any problems while your loan was being processed or during the repairs to your home?

Rock Island ➢ Rock Island uses a procedure and questionnaire similar to Charlotte's. If the completed homeowner's rating form indicates problems with the contractor, a copy of the evaluation is filed in the contractor's file. City staff discuss any problems found with the individual contractor to encourage correction in future work. These forms also help to provide documented evidence if the agency determines that a contractor should be removed from the list of contractors.

Charlotte ➤ Charlotte evaluates service contractors after nine months of one-year contracts in order to provide agency management with information for contract renewal decisions. The evaluations have enabled the agency to document poor performance of contractors. In one such situation, the contractor was a minority, a very sensitive issue in the city at that time. The city council did not renew the contract, based in large part on the extensive evaluation documentation.

For housing rehabilitation contracts, CDAs should also consider undertaking a follow-up evaluation before the end of the normal one-year warranty period. Problems in rehabilitation work may not show up for many months. This assessment can be undertaken by a telephone interview with the homeowner, sending the homeowner a questionnaire, or by actually visiting the home to look over the work and talk to the homeowner about any problems that have occurred. If a problem is found that is covered by the warranty, corrective action can be initiated.

Rock Island ➤ In Rock Island, in the final month before the warranty on rehab projects has expired, the construction officer visits the home and asks the homeowner if there are any problems with the work. If the homeowner identifies problems that the construction officer agrees are related to the contracted work, the construction officer contacts the contractors to get the corrections made.

This kind of follow-up can be particularly helpful to customers who may have forgotten or never really understood the warranty protection clauses, or who may not feel comfortable complaining to the agency or contractor.

For service contractors, CDAs should consider surveying at least a sample of clients served by the contractor. Administering a questionnaire that asks clients to assess the services they received is likely to be an appropriate evaluation procedure for most contracts in which the contractor works directly with citizens or individual businesses. Client feedback has an important secondary benefit: it indicates to customers that the CDA is interested in and listens to its customers.

Client questionnaires for service programs should include questions that ask for ratings of the quality of the service received, its helpfulness, its impact on the problems for which they sought help, its timeliness, and its accessibility.

In addition, open-ended questions can also be included, asking respondents to identify reasons for giving any poor ratings, any problems they encountered not covered elsewhere in the questionnaire, and suggestions for ways to improve the program.

The appropriate timing for questionnaire administration will depend on the objective of the specific service. For most services, surveys should be administered to clients shortly after service provision has been completed. For services intended to have a long-term impact, follow-up surveys should also be administered at a later point—perhaps 12 months or more after completion of service delivery.

Fairfax County ➤ To evaluate housing counseling and placement service contracts, Fairfax County is doing follow-up interviews 6 and 12 months after clients have received service to see whether placements have really been "permanent." The procedures include telephone interviews with former clients; mailing questionnaires to clients that cannot be reached by telephone; and telephone calls to landlords of non-respondents to determine if the client still resides at the location.

Some CDAs may need to have contractors survey their own clients because of the CDA's own resource constraints. This is especially the case with contracts that have large numbers of clients. Having contractors survey their own clients for the purpose of contract evaluation has several drawbacks. For example, the contractor may be tempted to manipulate the findings prior to providing them to the CDA. In addition, clients might feel inhibited about providing negative feedback directly to the service provider. Having contractors conduct their surveys can also add to the cost of the contract.

To reduce validity problems, the CDA would need to specify, or at least have the contractor agree on, survey procedures, including the wording of the questionnaire and sampling procedures to be used. The completed questionnaires might be mailed from the client directly to the CDA to reduce potential inhibition. Having contractors administer surveys has the advantage that the contractor can get ongoing feedback from clients and, therefore, might be more encouraged to respond to customer concerns. In general, surveying clients is a good internal management procedure for any service provider. Thus, CDAs should probably encourage contractors to survey their clients to help contractors improve their services.

Charlotte ➤ In Charlotte, a contractor for its family housing services program annually sends a questionnaire to all clients who have used its services the previous year or who are currently using them. This information is tallied by the contractor to identify the strengths and weaknesses of the program, and provided to the CDA. The evaluation form is brief, containing 11 questions on one page (see exhibit 6.6).

EXHIBIT 6.6

Family Housing Services, Inc., Client Evaluation of Counseling Session

Date ———————————— Next Appointment ————————————

Client Name ———————————— Address ————————————

Counselor Name ———————————— Your Telephone Number ————————————

	Yes	No	Not Sure
1. Do you understand what Family Housing Services does?			
2. Do you think Family Housing Services can help you solve your problem? If not why?			
3. Was your counselor courteous?			
4. Do you feel good about how Family Housing Services can help you? Comments			
5. Do you feel relieved that you have found help from Family Housing Services?			
6. Do you feel the counselor understood your problems?			
7. Were all your questions answered?			
8. Would you refer others to Family Housing Services?			
9. Was your session too long? Was your session too short?			
10. Do you plan to come to your next appointment?			
11. Were you comfortable in talking and working with your counselor?			

Additional Comments

————————————

Source: Charlotte, North Carolina, Community Development Department, 1990.

Resources Required to Implement these Ideas

Some of these ideas involve only administrative changes and do not require substantial change in organization or major new resources. For example, many of the suggestions regarding performance and incentive contracting are ideas for changing contract requirements. The CDA, however, will need to do follow-up monitoring and evaluation, which may cause an increase in cost. However, some monitoring and evaluation are a necessary component of administration for *any* contracts.

For actions such as providing technical assistance to contractors, a CDA needs to have qualified personnel available. In the absence of such staff support, the CDA will need help from private sources such as businesses or nonprofit agencies.

Some ideas presented here involve more effort on the part of the CDA. Many of the suggestions under monitoring and evaluation require a change in the status quo. For example, CDAs would have to prepare and file contractor evaluation reports and consider past performance in deciding on future contract awards. The extra time and effort to undertake the more extensive monitoring and evaluation suggested here, especially the customer feedback procedures, are somewhat foreign to most CDAs.

While sophisticated survey procedures are conceptually desirable, they are likely to be overly costly for other than large CDAs with healthy financial resources. Fortunately, "bargain basement" approaches can be used for most CDA purposes. For example, in very small as well as large CDAs, mailed or in-person questionnaires can be readily administered to housing rehab clients and service program clients by CDA inspectors or monitors. Thus, small agency size and even poor financial situations do not appear to be sufficient reasons for lack of comprehensive monitoring and evaluation of contractors.

7

Working Smarter: Making More Efficient Use of Resources

7.3(a)   Encourage staff members periodically to review agency procedures and work processes

7.3(b)   Provide training in productivity improvement

7.3(c)   Have outside staff independently take a fresh look at agency processes

7.3(d)   Streamline procedures and decentralize authority

7.3(e)   Provide recognition for successful productivity improvement efforts

ACTION 7.4   *Design Programs to Use Volunteers to Help Implement Services*

ACTION 7.5   *Periodically Evaluate Agency Programs to Identify Improvement Needs*

Working Smarter: Making More Efficient Use of Resources

Finding ways to make more efficient use of limited resources is a basic feature of management excellence. This chapter describes ideas and practices that will directly and indirectly lead to more efficient use of resources.

ACTION 7.1

Annually Set Objectives and Track Progress Toward Them
(Primary sources: Charlotte, North Carolina; Knoxville, Tennessee; Long Beach, California)

Setting objectives and tracking progress towards them helps promote more efficient use of resources because it focuses employee efforts and agency resources on the goals the agency wants to accomplish. Tracking progress toward achieving objectives enables the CDA to take corrective steps at an early stage if problems arise. The objective-setting process should include developing a plan for how to achieve the objectives, discussed under Action 7.2.

7.1(a)   *Develop quantity and quality targets for each objective*

Specific, measurable, results-oriented performance indicators and targets should be identified for each objective. The indicators and targets should be numerical wherever possible, rather than vague statements that cannot be tracked. Completion dates can be used as targets for objectives involving performance of specific tasks. Targets should be specified for each quarterly or monthly reporting period used by the CDA. Appendix B contains an illustrative list of performance indicators for a number of CDA programs. This list can be used as a starting point for CDA staff to select indicators applicable to their local situation. The appendix also indicates the likely data source for each indicator.

Both *quality* and *quantity* indicators should be chosen. For example, for a housing rehabilitation program, targets should include both the number of homes rehabilitated and measures of the quality, timeliness, and trouble-free nature of those rehabs. Indicators of quality are not frequently used by CDAs. This step involves procedures such as special tabulations of agency data (such as computing the time it took to complete rehabilitation), and surveys of agency clients to obtain feedback on program performance. Introducing and using such procedures will likely require added agency staff time and resources. Ways to measure service quality are discussed under Action 7.5.

Below are some examples of performance indicators and targets used for several of Charlotte's CDA activities.

Charlotte ➤ *Housing rehab*

— Complete rehab inspections within 5 days of assignment;

— Complete 75% of rehab work writeups and cost estimates within 5 days of initial inspection; complete 95% within 10 days.

Code enforcement:

— Correct 100% of dangerous violations within 120 days of initial inspection.

Housing relocation:

— Ensure that 75% of assisted moves take place within 9 months and that replacement housing is decent, safe, sanitary, and affordable;

— Ensure that an average of at least 15 households per relocation worker are moved to standard housing within the fiscal year.

Economic development:

— Create one job for a qualified low-income person for each $15,000 loaned from the economic development revolving loan fund.

In addition to targets focused on a program as a whole, CDAs can also develop productivity objectives for individual staff members or groups of employees. This is particularly useful for CDAs emphasizing productivity improvement because: it makes productivity improvement "part of the job" and increases employee awareness of and involvement in it; it demonstrates that upper management takes productivity improvement seriously; and it facilitates monitoring and evaluation of productivity at each level in the organization.

This will require time by management to communicate and discuss with employees their specific performance objectives, to track and monitor progress, and possibly to provide training in productivity improvement measures. Employees may feel that management is trying to squeeze more work out of them without extra rewards. To alleviate the latter problem, emphasis should be placed on "working smarter, not harder" and on how productivity improvement can lead to work simplification. Providing special recognition for successful efforts can also help.

Productivity targets might be stated in terms of the results of efforts, such as the planned reductions in time and cost or planned increases in output or service quality, or completion of specific productivity improvement projects, without specifying the amount of improvement expected. In the latter case, performance targets should include specific dates by which each target should be met. The following illustrate each of these approaches:

1. "Reduce the number of employee hours per unit of output by at least X percent during the next year" or, alternatively, "Increase the number of units of output by at least X percent during the next year." This form is rarely used by CDAs, probably because of the difficulties in determining what targets are reasonable.

2. "Complete a project to streamline activity Y by the end of the year." Charlotte, for example, included in its 1989-90 objectives: "Streamline reporting system," "Implement most efficient system for accounting and collection of loans," and "Improve the rehabilitation flow process and shorten the approval time."

7.1(b) *Use a collaborative process to obtain staff input on objectives and targets*

Those responsible for meeting objectives should participate in setting the objectives and targets. In addition, managers establishing targets for themselves should consult with their staff as well as their own supervisor to obtain input and ideas. If the targets will apply to non-management employees, these employees should have a say in setting them. This will encourage staff buy-in, increasing the likelihood of support for target achievement by all concerned. The next-higher level manager should be involved to ascertain that the objectives and targets reflect divisional and department objectives and that the targets are meaningful and realistic.

Long Beach ➤ Long Beach managers were given a copy of their supervisors' targets before developing their own performance measures. This was done to ensure that the performance measures and targets selected would be compatible with those of upper-level management.

Charlotte ➤ In Charlotte, the city's 1990 overall objectives for the CDA rehabilitation section included "Relocating into standard housing at least 15 households per relocation worker on the average" and "Completing an average of 45 rehabilitation jobs per inspector." These department-wide objectives were also translated into *individual staff* objectives. For example, the housing relocation specialists, as a group, set their own standard of having "on an average two clients successfully relocated each month into standard housing." This translates into an average of 24 households relocated per year.

This participation will make staff likely to be motivated to meet objectives, and will avoid the "not invented here" syndrome. Sometimes, however, political reality will intrude and targets will be established by the city or county council or by the agency head. This should be discussed with staff so that even if they don't like the targets, they will at least understand that "external" forces are involved.

On occasions where non-supervisory staff with similar jobs participate in setting their own performance targets, employees should establish group targets. The group may agree that some individuals have different assignments or clientele, warranting somewhat different targets. The group effort, however, will likely make each individual more comfortable with the resulting targets.

Charlotte ➤ In Charlotte, staff in the same job classification (such as code enforcement officers) met jointly with their supervisor to design the year's performance objectives for that job classification.

7.1(c)   *Set performance targets for most, if not all, activities and staff*

Objective-setting should be a task for most, if not all, CDA employees and should cover most activities. "Routine" activities should not be omitted. Some performance targeting systems have focused on innovations and special programs rather on regular activities. This led the staff performing routine activities at one CDA to feel their activities were less important to upper-level management, leading to lower employee morale and less attention paid to improving performance.

Most, or all, staff should also have objectives. Setting targets for *groups* or teams of employees encourages teamwork and encourages individuals not performing up to par to improve their performance. Targets for *individual* non-supervisory staff are more appropriate where individuals have clear-cut responsibilities and work independently, such as the case with staff working in different locations. Individual targets have the advantage of clearly designating responsibility, thus have the most motivational value. However, such targets can lead to lack of teamwork if individuals become overly competitive with one another.

If the objective-setting process is handled properly, participation in it will help motivate staff and make them feel part of the overall agency effort. Once targets are set, be sure to communicate them to all involved staff! Suggestions for setting objectives and targets are listed in exhibit 7.1.

Knoxville and Long Beach ➤ Both Knoxville and Long Beach agreed that to be most effective, the performance indicators and targets for each work unit and targets for the *whole department* should be communicated among all staff. As one Long Beach manager said, "Don't keep targets and their status a secret." This encourages staff and provides added incentive to staff to help meet targets.

7.1(d)   *Track objectives on a regular basis and provide timely progress reports to all parties involved*

Tracking objectives provides managers the opportunity to discuss progress with their staff. Exhibit 7.2 suggests steps for tracking performance.

Knoxville ➤ Knoxville informally and formally tracks and reviews progress toward objectives in its annual action plan. Section managers informally report on progress during their weekly meetings with the CDA director. The director and section managers informally provide status reports to all employees at monthly staff meetings. There is also a formal quarterly review of progress. For this review, section managers submit written status reports to the director, and progress is reviewed at a meeting of all section managers.

EXHIBIT 7.1

Suggestions for Setting Objectives and Targets

1. Give staff real input into setting the objectives and targets that apply to their work.

2. Use specific numerical targets, not vague, general ones that cannot be measured. For objectives involving completion of specific tasks, completion dates can be used as the targets.

3. Link targets to a plan for how they will be achieved. This will focus attention on "action" in reaching the targets rather than solely on the targets themselves.

4. Be sure the targets for each objective are realistic. Consider the human and financial resources available.

5. To establish targets, start with past performance and make adjustments based on resources and planned future actions. Past performance can indicate weaknesses and strengths, factors influencing performance, and potential recurring situations to watch out for.

6. Set targets for each reporting period, not only for the whole year. Consider seasonal factors and other timing considerations such as an expected surge of clients needing relocation during a particular period.

7. Avoid setting too many objectives. There is only so much information that an individual can handle. A limit of 6 to 10 objectives is likely to be manageable for each individual.

Charlotte ➤ In Charlotte, supervisors regularly check progress with each of their staff members (such as rehab or code enforcement specialists) and submit monthly reports to their division chief. The division chief meets with section chiefs and senior inspectors to review progress and to identify problems and ways to resolve them.

Charlotte ➤ Because Charlotte makes heavy use of numerical targets in its objective setting process, it has developed a computerized tracking system for a number of its programs. For code enforcement cases, for example, the computer tracks the time elapsed between specific events, and average times for activities. These can be compared against the objectives both overall and for individual inspectors. The computer printout also flags enforcement cases that are behind schedule.

Regular tracking permits identification of problems at an early stage. It also provides an opportunity for the employee to explain the causes of problems and plan potential solutions. The tracking process should be handled in a constructive way. When an individual or group

---

EXHIBIT 7.2

Suggestions for Tracking Performance on Objectives and Action Plans

1. Collect data on each performance indicator at regular quarterly or monthly intervals.

2. On the performance reports, compare actual progress on each performance indicator to the targets.

3. Signal for attention those indicators for which performance has fallen significantly behind or ahead of targets.

4. Ask organizational units to identify reasons for substantially under- or overachieving targets. Give the responsible unit the opportunity to review the results for each reporting period, provide explanations, and indicate proposed corrective actions *before* the progress report is submitted to upper level management.

5. Disseminate these reports to managers and staff throughout the organization.

6. Use instances where targets are not being met as an opportunity to identify problems and provide assistance to the unit responsible.

7. Review progress periodically with staff. Include the various objectives, actions, and performance levels in these reviews. Hold "how are we doing" sessions with staff after each performance report is issued.

8. Provide recognition for good performance, after each reporting period and at the year's end.

9. Keep objectives and action plans up-to-date by providing a process for necessary modifications.

---

has not met a target for a reporting period, the focus should be on identifying the problems and how to alleviate them, not on assigning blame. Staff should also be recognized for good performance after each reporting period and at the end of the year.

Timely reports on progress in meeting targets should be provided to the manager, the manager's supervisor(s), and the staff responsible for the objectives. The distribution of regular performance reports illustrates management's interest in the targets and that management takes them seriously.

Charlotte ➤ In addition to regular reports to staff, supervisors and managers, Charlotte's formal mid-year and year-end reports are provided to the director of the CDA, the director of the city's Budget and Evaluation Division and the City Manager. (Charlotte's objective setting process is a city-wide effort.)

Before providing performance reports to upper management, give the responsible manager and staff the opportunity to provide information about deficiencies (including external factors outside their control) and plans to correct them. This procedure will make the reporting process less threatening to staff and as noted above, will encourage them to look for reasons why performance is below targets.

Reports should be at least quarterly, if not monthly, and should be provided as soon as possible after the end of the reporting period, generally within one to two weeks. This will encourage staff to take prompt action if warranted. All persons involved with the delivery of a service whose objectives are being reported should receive a copy of the report. As an option, particularly for non-management personnel, reports might be posted in a location where they can be readily seen by those personnel.

Charlotte ➢ Charlotte posts monthly activity reports on bulletin boards. The report shows production and timeliness information related to each objective. For example, for code enforcement staff, the report shows the number of inspections and the length of time for completion for each inspector.

7.1(e) *Use the annual performance appraisal process as a time to assess progress on objectives and encourage continued attention to improvement*

The performance appraisal interview between the individual and supervisor is likely to be more constructive and easier for both parties if the discussion focuses on objective measures of progress. This is particularly so if the employee played a major role in setting the targets.

Charlotte ➢ Managers in Charlotte believe that having data from progress reports for each supervisor and inspector makes the task of conducting performance appraisals easier. Since the data are provided to staff members throughout the year, any problems discussed at the appraisal do not come as a surprise to the staff member.

7.1(f) *Provide an opportunity for staff to suggest modifications to objectives and/or targets if circumstances warrant*

In our interviews, we found that nothing turned staff off more than their perception that they were responsible for meeting targets that were no longer attainable, due to changes in circumstances since the targets were initially set.

For example, changing economic conditions might prevent a redevelopment effort from proceeding, or there might be major changes in funding. When such circumstances occur, previous objectives or targets can become obsolete. If something is not done, staff may become de-motivated because they feel it is impossible to meet the original targets.

Charlotte ➤ CDA staff in Charlotte were unable to meet some of their objectives in 1989 because of Hurricane Hugo, which caused considerable added workload for agency staff.

If circumstances change *substantially* in a way that significantly affects the ability of staff to achieve one or more of their objectives, agency managers should examine the objectives to determine whether some should be modified, deleted, or marked as no longer applicable, whether new ones should be added, or whether they should be retained because they are city-wide political objectives that cannot be deleted. In the last case, explanations can be attached as to why the targets cannot be achieved. The agency should have explicit rules for modifying targets. For example, the manager who identifies the change should document why it is needed, then obtain agreement of upper-level management.

Ideally, the affected staff and their supervisor should be allowed to set revised targets for the remainder of the year, even if these new targets are only reported internally.

These steps can greatly reduce staff concern and anger over what they believe are unfair objectives. Staff who feel they have been heard, even if their requests were turned down, are likely to remain supportive of the process and the objectives.

ACTION 7.2

> ## Develop and Track Action Plans
>
> (Primary sources: Knoxville, Tennessee; Long Beach, California)

There are many advantages to attaching the process of annual objective setting to development of an action plan for the year. First, it will make the objectives more realistic. Second, action planning contributes to efficient use of resources by focusing resources on the goals the CDA wants to accomplish. Ideally, action plans should be prepared as part of the objective-setting process. Action plans are one way to help ensure that objectives will be carried out. Each objective may require one or several actions during the year to accomplish; these should be specified in the action plan.

The action planning process also gives staff the opportunity to reexamine their programs and consider more efficient ways of delivering their services. Agency staff have the opportunity to do advance thinking and be proactive, not merely reactive. During the rest of the year, staff are likely to have their hands full just responding to day-to-day demands. Thus, action plans are both an employee motivation procedure and a way to plan for the year, encourage action, and hold managers accountable for performance.

Action plans should include the following components:

— A statement of the agency's and of individual manager's objectives;

— A listing of the major activities to carry out during the coming year to meet each objective;

— Identification of the manager or unit responsible for each activity;

— Specific targets for each activity, including specific performance indicator(s) such as quantities or schedule dates;

— The planned budget and staff resources for each activity.

The reader should refer to Action 7.1, above, for discussion of development of objectives and targets.

7.2(a) *Tie the action plan to both dollar and staff resource considerations*

Action plans are realistic only if they reflect financial and staff resources available for each objective.

The action plan should be used by the CDA to help develop its annual budget, and should be linked to the budget preparation process. It will be most useful if it is designed for the agency's fiscal rather than calendar year, so that it can be closely linked to expected agency resources.

The action plan can then also be used as part of the agency's budget justification. The plan, however, will need to be reviewed and modified as necessary after the final budget has been passed, and should be considered a draft until then.

Knoxville and Long Beach ➤ Both Knoxville and Long Beach felt that the best time to develop an action plan and establish performance targets was as a precursor to the budget process. Establishing the plan, objectives, and targets acted as a planning activity leading to development of their proposed budgets.

Alternatively, the CDA might prepare the action plan shortly *after* the budget has been passed by the local government. This timing still permits the plan to be used to help motivate employees and to provide a way to track progress. However, this approach relinquishes the plan's usefulness in helping develop and justify the agency's budget.

7.2(b)   *Include action planning as part of annual staff retreats*

If the CDA holds staff retreats (see chapter 5), the agency's annual action plan is an appropriate subject for the retreat. Developing the plan at a staff retreat has the benefit of getting all staff involved in establishing and implementing the plan.

Action plans, however, cannot be completed at a retreat. Advance work and post-retreat modifications are likely to be necessary.

Knoxville   ➤ Knoxville's CDA makes action plan preparation the major activity at its annual two-day, all-staff retreat in early February. Individual divisions of the agency work separately on their own components of the plan. At the end of the retreat, the divisions report to each other on what they have produced. After the retreat, the divisions make revisions as needed until the action plan is finalized after the budget is approved by the city council.

ACTION 7.3

Encourage Continuing Productivity Improvement Efforts
(Primary sources: Charlotte, North Carolina; Knoxville, Tennessee; Pinellas County, Florida; Santa Ana, California)

Encouraging productivity improvement is closely linked to more efficient use of resources. This section describes a variety of approaches that CDAs can use to encourage productivity improvement.

One basic way to foster staff attention to productivity improvement is to show that management is interested in it. There are several ways to do this.

As discussed in chapter 5, managers should encourage staff to suggest changes to current procedures, take time to listen to their suggestions, and give them full consideration. If, after full consideration the suggestion does not appear worthwhile, management should explain the reasons for the rejection (in a tactful way) and encourage future suggestions. If management works with, and listens to staff, positive and productive changes can take place and a greater sense of pride can be created.

Knoxville ➤ In Knoxville, the eight code enforcement officers, the secretary/records specialist, and the code enforcement manager together worked out a process for expediting code enforcement paperwork. They developed a single, computer-integrated form to be completed based on information inspectors phoned in. This reduced the amount of paperwork, the backlog of code complaints, and the time that a complaint stays on the backlog list. Violation notices are now generated by computer, which has reduced the time required to send notices to violators. To develop these new procedures, the code enforcement manager met with the code enforcement and clerical personnel in a number of early morning sessions. Staff flow-charted the current procedures and designed the new ones. The employees had been pushing this streamlining suggestion for years, but it was the current management that listened and implemented it.

Another way to promote productivity improvement is to include productivity improvement objectives as part of the agency's objective setting process (discussed above under Action 7.1 (a)), as done in Charlotte. In addition, managers can include a phrase such as "improving service quality and finding better, more efficient ways to use agency resources" in the position descriptions for all supervisory personnel. Similar responsibilities might also be included in the position descriptions for senior professional staff, such as rehabilitation inspectors, loan officers, and economic development specialists. This will highlight productivity improvement as an integral part of job activities.

7.3(a) *Encourage staff members periodically to review agency procedures and work processes*

Periodic review of each program encourages staff to look afresh at their work. Reviews might be done every one to two years. More frequent reviews are probably not necessary, since situations are not likely to have changed sufficiently to warrant another look. However, when circumstances change significantly, such as if important personnel changes or program modifications are made, these are good opportunities for reviews.

Staff should be encouraged to suggest small improvements, not only "blockbusters." Many small improvements can amount to significant increases in efficiency.

Brainstorming can be used to encourage personnel to identify possible new ways to deliver CDA services. This might be tried periodically at regular staff meetings, or as one component of a staff retreat.

One way to organize productivity improvement reviews is by using problem-solving work groups or teams to critically examine work procedures and recommend improvements (see chapter 5). Problem-solving teams, such as "quality teams," are often used in the context of city- or county-wide productivity or quality improvement efforts. However, they can also be adopted by a CDA.

Pinellas County ➤ Pinellas County initiated a "Quality Improvement" process for all county agencies, which focused on improving the quality of service to the community. The CDA's 19-person staff was grouped into three teams: (1) "Wheels of Fortune" (named for the building in which the CDA is located), consisting of administrative and office staff; (2)"Reg Runners," consisting of compliance staff; and (3)"Unisix" (so named because there are six members in the team), consisting of rehab staff. Team names—particularly catchy or humorous ones—build team spirit and employee motivation. Team captains received intensive training for 5 days on various tools and techniques such as data gathering and analysis, brainstorming, and action plans. Some of the initial improvements the teams made include:

— Setting up a "forms cabinet" so that each staff member has a place to receive and distribute information. The cabinet is centrally located in the CDA office. Previously, distributing mail and routing material required legwork for each individual office. The new process saves time and is more efficient.

— Computers are now used for messages or bulletins that need to be sent simultaneously to all or many staff members. Previously, "word of mouth" and posting of notices were used.

Santa Ana introduced a quality improvement process using problem-solving teams. The initial efforts of the CDA's rehab team resulted in better use of supervisory time and improved service to customers.

Santa Ana ➤ Santa Ana's housing rehab "quality team" first chose to analyze the loan review/approval process. The team prepared a flow chart of the process and then graphed the time required for each of the stages (based on a random sample of 30 cases). This helped the team identify the stages where delays occurred. Team members then considered ways to shorten the times. Based on the team's review, the process of assigning inspections was changed. Previously, crew supervisors reviewed each case and assigned it to a specialist. Now inspections are assigned on a rotating basis by a support staff member, saving supervisor time and speeding up the process. (Cases are still specially assigned under some circumstances, such as if the homeowner speaks only Spanish, or if a specialist is too far behind in previous work.) Because of their team analysis, Santa Ana rehab staff developed a better understanding of the loan approval process. As a result, rehab staff were better able to work together and to shorten the amount of time needed to process approvals. The combined effects reduced the amount of processing time from an average of 71 to 38 days.

Topics to be addressed might be selected by problem-solving groups themselves. This gives the groups maximum participation in the productivity improvement effort, but groups may select topics that management believes are unimportant and perhaps not worth the effort. (This has been a problem with the implementation of "quality circles" in many different government agencies.) Another approach is for management to identify the topic and ask a group to address it. A middle ground is for management to identify a basic concern, but allow the group to tackle the aspect of that concern that the group finds appropriate. In Santa Ana, management asked the housing rehab team to review the housing rehab program; the team selected loan processing time as its specific focus.

Problem-solving teams usually have the following characteristics (see chapter 5 for more detail):

— Membership is on a voluntary basis; all staff members in a given unit would not necessarily belong to the group.

— Teams include at least some staff members involved with the process being examined. Teams can also be organized so that all members are from the same unit or division. This contributes to group understanding of the process being analyzed, and facilitates implementation of recommendations.

— Group size is usually limited to 6-12 members to facilitate interaction.

— Teams generally meet on a regular basis while working on a particular productivity problem. Teams might disband or have some changes in membership after solving a specific problem. In other cases teams exist on a continuing basis, tackling new problems all the time. This on-going team format is often associated with "quality circles."

— Some special training in problem-solving and group process techniques is often provided to team members or leaders. Training is discussed under Action 7.3(b), below.

See chapter 5, Action 5.1(c) for the potential drawbacks of problem-solving teams.

7.3(b) *Provide training in productivity improvement*

Training is generally needed for staff members to function as problem-solving work groups described above. Training should cover the following elements (adapted from Santa Ana's experience—see chapter 5 for more detail):

❐ Flow-charting the sequence of the process being examined;

❐ Process analysis through basic statistical analysis, including random sampling;

❐ Ways to identify problems in the current process;

❐ Brainstorming and other ways to encourage creative thinking and identify options for improving the process and reducing the problem examined;

❐ Ways to gather data needed to analyze the various options, possibly including surveying other employees and customers;

❐ Ways to present findings and recommendations to management in a clear, concise, and organized way, both orally and in writing; and

❐ Procedures for subsequently following up on changes made to determine the extent to which the changes are beneficial or need modifications.

Training in productivity improvement methods is likely to be available from consultants or from faculty members at nearby universities or colleges. These sessions are likely to be costly, unless CDA personnel have good relations with faculty and can coax them into providing occasional sessions for CDA employees.

Other ways to provide training opportunities are the following:

❏ Send staff to professional meetings where they can learn about innovations used by other agencies. Many if not most CDAs already provide such opportunities, at least occasionally. This approach is particularly needed for agencies unable to make use of consultants or faculty members.

❏ Institute informal seminars for staff, perhaps formulated as "brown bag seminars" during lunch hour. These can involve informal presentations by CDA staff or staff from other agencies, who describe productivity/work simplification techniques that they initiated and found successful. On occasion, outside experts might be brought in to give similar briefings.

❏ Distribute or route articles on productivity improvement efforts undertaken elsewhere to supervisors or other appropriate staff members. See exhibit 7.3 for a handout, prepared and distributed by Charlotte's city manager that the CDA director found useful and, in turn, distributed to his own staff.

7.3(c) *Have outside staff independently take a fresh look at agency processes*

In cases where management believes that major improvements are needed, it may be desirable to have "outsiders" undertake analysis and recommendations. This approach is desirable if line staff do not have sufficient time to work in productivity improvement teams, if complex analytical techniques are required, such as developing or selecting major new technology, or if complex statistical techniques are needed to analyze work methods. In any event, procedures of each major program should be given an outside review every 4 to 5 years, a review that can be conducted more efficiently by outside specialists.

The independent analysts can be within the department, outside the department but from a central agency such as a central management analysis unit, or outside consultants. Some CDA officials feel that outside consultants are usually not effective because they lack knowledge of community development programs and the nuances of a particular agency. On the other hand, it is costly to have permanent special staff for such projects.

Even where a special unit is used to conduct work simplification studies, the agency should obtain the input of program staff as much as possible, so they do not perceive themselves as the "victims" of the study.

EXHIBIT 7.3

Example of Productivity Improvement Information

PRODUCTIVITY

The characteristics of productivity

Effective Use Of Resources Knowing and using all the resources available to accomplish a task or project with minimum wasted time, effort and materials.

Innovation As any task unfolds, inquiring into how it can be done better, faster and more satisfying for the customer.

Creativity Using imagination to overcome limited resources.

Involvement Staying in regular, harmonious communication with everyone around you. Paying attention to details and being alert to changes in your operating environment, new ideas and potential breakdowns.

Balance Always weighing the ideal of efficiency against the priority of effective customer service across a broad diversity of needs and expectations.

INITIAL IDEAS:

· Implement an incentive program to encourage and reward suggestions which improve service, save money or otherwise contribute to our mission.
· Establish a regular program in which immediate supervisors will honor exemplary acts of service by individual employees.
· Develop departmental and/or section groups to brainstorm productivity ideas (e.g., Quality Circles in industry).
· Enlist the support of businesses and universities in developing productivity improvements.
· Set up a City-wide "bulletin board" (electronic or printed) to share valuable ideas between departments.
· Include individuals at every level in setting and achieving departmental objectives. Do not compromise on objectives. Hold every objective as a promise to be kept, not a vague ideal to be "hit or missed."
· Train employees in creativity skills.
· Be sensitive to the relationship between family issues and productivity and develop leave policies, flex-time schedules, job sharing and work-at-home opportunities.
· Establish a structure and policy for sabbaticals.
· Encourage use of new technologies.

YOUR IDEAS:

_____
_____
_____
_____
_____
_____
_____
_____
_____
_____
_____
_____
_____
_____
_____

ADDITIONAL NOTES:

Source: City of Charlotte, North Carolina, 1989.

Charlotte ➤ Charlotte uses an internal agency staff group to undertake studies on occasion. A study of the housing rehabilitation and code enforcement program resulted in a major change: combining the rehabilitation specialist and code enforcement inspector jobs. Each group was cross trained in the other's job. The number of inspections and rehab jobs per inspector increased significantly over the next five years. (This arrangement, however, was recently changed back. The supervisors felt that the combination had run its course and had begun to diminish the quality of rehabilitation services because of increased specialization needs.)

7.3(d)   *Streamline procedures and decentralize authority*

Streamlining procedures and reducing paperwork increase productivity by enabling staff to spend more time providing services, and usually makes happier staff and customers. Decentralizing authority means that staff can more rapidly answer questions, make decisions, and resolve complaints. These steps reduce customer aggravation. In addition, they increase employees' feelings of importance and worth, encouraging them to treat the customer with greater attention and respect (see chapter 5 for further discussion of delegation and motivation).

Some risks are involved with decentralizing authority, particularly if it is pushed on employees too fast, without providing time to train them in the expanded responsibilities or more complex tasks. Managers and some staff may resist such changes, fearful that staff will make embarrassing mistakes. CDA management should let managers and staff know that some errors are an inevitable side effect of decentralization.

CDAs should periodically review program procedures to identify and implement opportunities to streamline activities. Such reviews can be done by managers themselves, by special problem-solving teams (see 7.3(a)), or by an internal staff unit that performs such functions (see 7.3(c)).

San Mateo County ➤ In San Mateo County, a special team was created to seek ways to simplify, combine, and computerize agency forms. Staff report that the team reduced the number of forms from 117 to 52.

One of the easiest ways to initiate simplification efforts is to have staff in each program or unit prepare a flow chart for each program or function. From this, the group can then search for steps that can be eliminated or combined, revised, or added in order to simplify or speed up the process. The following is an example of this approach:

Charlotte ➤ Charlotte's department head asked each section to flow-chart their work and look for ways to simplify and improve their processes. As a result of this process, the code enforcement group redesigned inspection reports to permit checking off responses, rather than having inspectors write down their comments. This reduced time spent writing and freed inspectors for more useful activities. The new form also enabled the computer to automatically print letters based on the information on the inspectors' worksheets. Code enforcement inspectors still check letters before they are mailed because computers can make mistakes.

Staff reviews do not require special technical procedures or outside consultants. However, training in flow charting, brainstorming, and group interaction are likely to be helpful, at least for some members of the group.

The following steps for work simplification were suggested by Charlotte's CDA staff:

1. Select a particular promising or important activity to review.

2. Get the facts on the present way the job is done.

3. Question each current step and list the possibilities for improvement.

4. Develop an alternative procedure, and test it to be sure it works and is an improvement.

5. Install and maintain so the new method continues to produce results.

7.3(e) *Provide recognition for successful productivity improvement efforts*

Employees need to feel that their productivity improvement suggestions are recognized and rewarded in some way. Otherwise, they are not likely to continue suggesting improvements.

While financial awards are one possibility, they present special difficulties, such as concerns over fairness. In addition, staff might come to expect extra payment for making suggestions to improve productivity, instead of feeling that this is a basic part of their job.

Non-financial recognition can often be just as effective. An obvious but often neglected action is for managers to informally compliment staff who have contributed ideas that have been implemented in the agency. Everyone appreciates a pat on the back from supervisors. Don't underestimate the importance of letting individual staff know you recognize their contributions.

Memos recording employees' contributions can be inserted in their files and considered during their performance appraisals as well.

The same techniques designed to increase employee involvement (see chapter 5, Action 5.4(a)) apply here to recognizing staff contributions to productivity improvement. Letters acknowledging employee suggestions should be sent where the suggestions are significant enough to warrant them. Similarly, letters should be sent to the mayor or city manager (with a copy to the employee) to recognize suggestions leading to significant improvements or savings.

Pinellas County   ➤   Pinellas County issues a newsletter called "Quality News" as part of its county-wide quality improvement effort. The newsletter provides updates on the Quality Improvement process in all departments. Individuals and teams are recognized for their accomplishments, and their procedures and techniques are described to allow others to use them. A CDA can do the same in its own agency newsletter.

CDAs can provide recognition through plaques, trophies, or T-shirts. Small prizes might be awarded for the best productivity improvement suggestion of the month or quarter. For example, awarding a box of doughnuts or a pizza to the team with the best idea for the month is a small but tangible form of recognition. Providing a "coupon" for a small amount of time off (a half-hour or hour, for example) is another way to reward good ideas. Care should be taken to develop a system for awarding prizes that is perceived as fair. A prize system should be discontinued if it appears to be generating jealousy or concerns about favoritism.

Pinellas County   ➤   In Pinellas County, quality improvement teams receive Q (for quality) stickers for each accomplishment. Accumulation of stickers makes teams eligible for various awards. For example, when a team receives its 10th Q sticker, each team member receives a coupon for 30 minutes of time off work. For their 20th sticker, each member receives a time off coupon and a pin. For the 25th sticker, team members receive a time off coupon and a plaque for their office or work site. The plaque is presented at a meeting of the Board of County Commissioners.

➤   Pinellas County also sponsors quarterly award presentations recognizing all team accomplishments. In addition, it makes annual presentations of gold, silver and bronze trophies in the following categories: teams with the most accomplishments; teams with the best accomplishments; teams whose accomplishments saved the most money; and teams whose accomplishments were the most creative. Names of annual winners are also displayed in the lobby of the Courthouse. Judging for these awards is done by a committee of County Administrator staff and/or community business professionals.

Problem-solving work teams are appropriate for all but small CDAs, which are already likely to be working as a team, if only for self-preservation. Problem-solving teams and other staff-generated improvement efforts are likely to be successful only in agencies where management fully encourages this approach. Upper management need to "sell" the team approach to first-line and middle-management in order for it to have a chance of succeeding.

If an agency's working atmosphere is poor, employee morale is low, and staff significantly mistrust management, pushing productivity might be counter-productive. In such cases, employees may feel the push is "to get more work out of them" without compensating for it. For such agencies, introducing these ideas should be put on the back burner until the atmosphere is improved, through focusing on the ideas presented in chapter 5.

ACTION 7.4

Design Programs to Use Volunteers to Help Implement Services

(Primary source: Cleveland, Ohio)

U sing citizen volunteers to partially or wholly implement programs is another way for CDAs to make more efficient use of resources. Volunteers can supplement agency staff, helping limited resources go further. However, staff resources will still be needed for volunteer supervision, assistance, recruitment, and training. CDAs already work with community volunteers through advisory groups and neighborhood organizations. In this section, we focus on volunteers helping CDAs undertake activities that staff would otherwise have to take on.

There are many advantages to using volunteers that go well beyond the financial savings involved. Working with citizens and neighborhood organization personnel as volunteers helps create among volunteers a greater sense of ownership and responsibility for their neighborhoods. This may translate into additional independent community development efforts. Volunteers are also likely be a good source of suggestions for improving the programs in which they participate. Volunteer involvement may help strengthen the neighborhood organization, as members and residents get to know each other through contact begun as part of the volunteer effort. Similarly, relations between the CDA and citizens will improve as staff get to know the volunteers better and develop cooperative working relationships with them. Staff are also likely to become more familiar with the neighborhoods involved in volunteer efforts.

Designing a program for delivery by volunteers may also increase use of the program by customers, who may feel more comfortable participating in it because other citizens are involved. Thus, volunteer participation may be viewed as a kind of citizen endorsement of the program. This may be particularly helpful for programs encouraging compliance or self-help efforts on the part of citizens—such as code enforcement, neighborhood clean-up or beautification, or crime prevention.

Use of volunteers also has potential drawbacks. Some volunteers may not perform their jobs well, and some may be unreliable. Staff members or unions may perceive volunteers as a threat to jobs. Thus, use of volunteers is likely to have increased appeal in situations where CDA cutbacks have previously occurred. Finally, some volunteers may be confronted or harassed by residents, particularly if they are working in compliance-related programs such as code enforcement.

Below is one example of an especially innovative use of volunteers in Cleveland:

Cleveland ➤ Cleveland's Neighborhood Code Enforcement Partnership Program, operated by the CDA's Building and Housing Division (BHD), uses volunteers to perform external inspections of property for minor code violations. The program involves neighborhood organizations in recruiting and managing volunteers. It began in 1986 after budget cuts reduced code enforcement staff, causing the city to cut back on inspections *not* related to a complaint. Using volunteers was a way to maintain these inspections despite declining budgets.

➤ The program is used in neighborhoods with moderate deterioration with the goal of voluntary correction of minor code violations. Volunteers use a checklist to identify minor code violations for each property inspected. (Major violations are referred to BHD using a regular complaint form.) The checklist identifying the home's minor violations is sent to the homeowner with a cover letter explaining the program (see exhibit 7.4) and indicating that a formal inspection will be required if conditions are not improved. Volunteers also re-inspect the property about three months later to see if conditions have been corrected.

EXHIBIT 7.4

Example of Letter Explaining Volunteer Program to Residents

**BUCKEYE
AREA DEVELOPMENT
CORPORATION**

DEPARTMENT OF COMMUNITY DEVELOPMENT
CHRISTOPHER P. WARREN
Director

DIVISION OF BUILDING & HOUSING
MIR LAIK ALI
Commissioner

MICHAEL R. WHITE
Mayor

JAY WESTBROOK
President, City Council

Dear Neighbor,

The purpose of this letter is to introduce the Neighborhood Code Enforcement Partnership Program (NCEPP), a combined effort between the City of Cleveland, Division of Building and Housing and the Buckeye Area Development Corporation (BADC) to encourge voluntary home repairs and improve housing maintenance.

Your street has been surveyed by trained neighborhood volunteers to determine exterior housing and yard conditions. The volunteers have received special training and information about Code Violations which enables them to identify these conditions. Enclosed is a copy of the survey completed for your house. Those items marked indicate problem areas which we encourage you to voluntarily repair within ninety (90) days.

The BADC will work to contact each homeowner to discuss the survey and the available resources to assist them. Also please find enclosed a brochure describing the housing programs available in the Buckeye area. A formal inspection by a City Inspector, which could result in a violation notice from the Division of Building and Housing, will be necessary only if the conditions in the survey are not voluntarily corrected by the specified time. The neighborhood will be surveyed again to determine the success of the program in stimulating repairs.

The NCEPP grew out of the need for voluntary code compliance involving neighborhood people. If you are interested in volunteering please call the BADC office - 491-8450.

If you have additional questions for the Division of Building and Housing, please contact Jayne M. Zborovsky, the Partnership Director at 664-2834, or James Kocian, NCEPP Administrative Officer at 664-4361.

We are looking forward to working with you. A key factor in increased property values is the exterior condition and maintenance of your house. The BADC is offering a free safety lamppost to those homes who comply with the housing code. Please help us in making New Buckeye a Reality!

Sincerely yours,

Mir Laik Ali, Commissioner   James A. Sipos, Executive Director
Division of Building and Housing   Buckeye Area Development Corporation

Source: Cleveland, Ohio, Department of Community Development, 1990.

If not, another warning letter is sent. Volunteers attempt to call the homeowner to inform them of programs that can help them repair their property and urge them to make repairs if they have not already done so.

➤ Cleveland's program grew from six participating organizations and 30-40 volunteers in 1986 to 29 organizations and 165 volunteers in 1989. BHD estimates 14,000 volunteer hours were contributed in 1989, and over 9,000 inspections were made, including follow-up inspections. The compliance rate ranges from 60 to 90 percent in various neighborhoods. BHD also estimates that there is a 2 to 1 ratio of private dollars for improvements in areas participating in the program. Another benefit is that government is being proactive in dealing with code violations, rather than waiting for complaints to be made.

The following suggestions for developing a volunteer program are based on Cleveland's experience.

1. Get input and support from representatives of the groups expected to be affected by or involved in the volunteer effort. Such participation will be helpful in developing the program and should also increase support for it. Cleveland used a task force that included neighborhood representatives, code enforcement inspectors, building and housing division staff members, neighborhood planners, and representatives of residential and commercial neighborhood organizations participating in the program. Neighborhood organizations participating in the program are required to pass a board resolution stating their support.

2. Seek legal advice about how to use volunteers to avoid legal difficulties. In Cleveland, CDA staff consulted the city's legal department. To avoid legal problems their code enforcement volunteers are required to stay on sidewalks or in alleyways.

3. Introduce volunteer programs on a pilot basis in a limited number of areas. Success in pilot efforts will help sell the program. Cleveland's code enforcement volunteer program was introduced in six areas where the neighborhood organizations and council members were supportive of it. The program was subsequently expanded to 29 areas.

4. Explain the program to staff members and unions (if applicable) when it is introduced, and include it in introductory/training information provided to new employees. If possible, provide assurances that volunteers will not cause reduction in paid staff. Involve the CDA director in introducing the program to other CDA managers and staff.

5. Make presentations to the mayor, county executive, and council members to introduce the program and its purpose. In Cleveland the staff member in charge of the program was a former council member, which helped her sell the program to other council members. It is helpful to have an elected official introduce the program to other elected officials.

6. Use the media to introduce the program to the general public. Use press releases promoting the positive features of the volunteer program, for example, that code enforcement helps improve neighborhood conditions.

7. Send letters to residents of areas where the volunteer activity will take place to explain the program. This will allay concerns of residents, and should reduce the likelihood of confrontations with volunteers. Send such a letter from the participating neighborhood organization as done in Cleveland (see exhibit 7.4). Notify the police if volunteers will be performing tasks that residents might view as suspicious and report to the police.

8. Develop checklists and forms for volunteers to use.

9. Provide training for all volunteers. Cleveland provides three training sessions and a minimum of 10 hours of training. The first session introduces the program and the forms used; the second is a slide show/lecture on code violations; the third describes field practices. Personnel from participating neighborhood organizations attend the training sessions with the volunteers. The training process should include:

   a. Written and graphic materials. Cleveland developed a training package that describes different kinds of code violations, including drawings of a house showing code violation conditions to look for.

   b. Slides or videos. Cleveland uses a 50-minute slide show developed by code enforcement staff to illustrate various minor and major code enforcement violations.

   c. At least one hands-on training session at which volunteers demonstrate their capabilities before being allowed to work alone. In Cleveland, after volunteers have seen the slide show on code enforcement, small groups go into the field with code enforcement personnel for a 3 to 4 hour training session to practice using the checklist. This training session provides an opportunity for questions and answers, as well as observation of the volunteers. If staff feel any volunteers lack a good understanding of the training provided, they will repeat the slide show and hold another field training session.

d. Refresher training as needed. Cleveland's code enforcement staff provide refresher training for volunteers on request.

10. Provide staff support to oversee volunteer efforts. CDA staff can be supplemented by personnel from neighborhood organizations involved in the volunteer effort. A CDA staff member is project director of Cleveland's code enforcement partnership, and several code enforcement inspectors are also assigned to this program. Each is assigned to 2 to 3 partnership areas, primarily to work on code enforcement of major violations but also to oversee volunteer efforts. These inspectors have monthly meetings with the neighborhood organizations that manage the volunteer efforts. Neighborhood organization personnel participating in the Cleveland code enforcement partnership manage the volunteer effort in their area. This includes assigning volunteers to teams, assigning territories to cover, and making monthly follow-up calls to be sure volunteers are covering the areas assigned, that they are continuing to perform the amount of work they agreed to, and to ask if they are having any problems or need additional training. The neighborhood organizations provide volunteers with the checklist and review them for completeness once handed in.

11. Recruit volunteers. Staff should help recruit volunteers by making presentations to neighborhood organizations interested in participating in the program. This is Cleveland's primary method of recruiting for the program. Cleveland also distributes brochures and provides extra copies to the neighborhood organizations to give to interested residents.

12. Answer volunteers' questions and help resolve problems. Volunteers should be encouraged to contact CDA staff or neighborhood organization personnel if they have questions, or want refresher training, or if they feel unsure of their skills and want a staff member to accompany them on one of their assignments.

13. Provide specific instructions to volunteers as to how they should handle problem situations. If someone challenges Cleveland's code enforcement volunteers, they are told to provide that person with the telephone number of the code enforcement department and move on to the next house.

14. Periodically monitor and do quality checks of each volunteer's work. A schedule for such quality control monitoring should be established and followed, with more frequent monitoring of new volunteers. Cleveland code inspectors check a sample of volunteers' checklists, and visit a sample of properties to see if they have been correctly rated. CDA staff can also observe them "in action," monitor complaints from citizens, and survey staff

members who have had contact with the volunteers to determine what changes may be needed.

15. Design volunteer efforts so they are a positive experience for the volunteer. This will encourage continued volunteer participation. For example:

    a. Encourage volunteers to work in teams of two or more, as done in Cleveland. It is helpful to team new volunteers with veterans. This provides companionship and makes volunteering a more pleasant experience. It provides someone to easily consult with if a volunteer is unsure about what to do in a given situation. It is also a safety measure for volunteers who are performing activities that might generate hostility or otherwise put them at risk.

    b. Have CDA staff meet regularly with volunteers to give them feedback on the results of their efforts and to provide encouragement and thanks.

    c. Recognize volunteer efforts by:

       — Holding recognition events such as annual luncheons or dinners where officials express their appreciation for volunteer efforts;

       — Encouraging neighborhood organizations that are involved in, or benefit from, the program to recognize volunteers in some way such as at receptions or in newsletters;

       — Presenting certificates, plaques, or token gifts. In Cleveland, a group photograph of staff and volunteers was taken and presented to volunteers.

       — Distributing occasional press releases that identify volunteers, particularly in neighborhood-focused or ethnic newspapers.

16. Evaluate the program on a regular basis (see Action 7.5 for suggestions on evaluation procedures).

Introducing a volunteer program is probably not feasible where there are unpleasant and volatile union/employee problems. Volunteers from outside an area should probably not be assigned to locations where CDA-community relations are poor.

Resource Requirements. Resources are required to manage and develop volunteer efforts, for instance, for supplies used in training efforts.

Cleveland ➤ Cleveland assigned 25 percent of a staff member's time to be project director for the volunteer program. On average, code enforcement inspectors assigned to this program spend about 10 to 15 percent of their time on the volunteer effort. This includes meeting with neighborhood organizations that operate the program and training and recruiting volunteers. The remainder of code enforcement staff time is spent on major code violations in the target areas. Each training program takes about 10 hours of time on the part of one code enforcement officer.

During the early stages of a volunteer program, the project director is likely to have to devote a substantial amount of time to the program. The Cleveland project director devoted 60 to 75 percent of her time during the program's early years. Introducing a volunteer program is probably not feasible when there are unpleasant and volatile union/employee problems. Volunteers should probably not be assigned to locations where CDA-community relations are poor.

ACTION 7.5

Periodically Evaluate Agency Programs to Identify Improvement Needs

(Primary sources: Albany, New York; Charlotte, North Carolina, Cuyahoga County, Ohio; Kansas City, Missouri; Long Beach, California; Rock Island, Illinois)

It is desirable to evaluate each major CDA program every 3 to 4 years.[1] Each CDA, however, will need to be selective in deciding when a program needs to be examined, such as when problems have been occurring regularly in service delivery or costs have been rising excessively, or when a new program manager comes in and wants the program reviewed. These are likely to be major opportunities for productive program evaluations.

Evaluations should assess not only procedures and processes, but also their impacts and resulting service quality. Action 6.6 in chapter 6 discusses evaluating the results of contracts and individual contractors. Here, the focus is on the overall results of a program, across all service providers. *Program evaluations should be used to guide decisions about the need for program modifications.*

To assess the impact of a program on the community, a variety of procedures and sources of information are likely to be needed. These include:

— Existing agency data. For example, the number of customers assisted and calculations of response time for services. Contract monitoring and evaluation reports in agency files will also be sources (see chapter 6).

— Feedback from customers obtained through carefully planned and administered surveys. Household and business customers can be asked about their experiences with specific agency programs, including their ratings of various program characteristics and their reasons for not being satisfied with particular aspects. Customers can also be asked for their suggestions for improving the program.

— "Trained observer" ratings to assess conditions. Program staff or others can be trained in the use of scales to rate particular physical characteristics such as the external condition of houses and business facilities and the physical appearance of neighborhoods.

Below are some suggestions on customer surveys and trained observer procedures.

Customer Survey Procedures

CDAs can survey all or a representative sample of program customers to ask about their experiences with the program. A detailed discussion of survey procedures is beyond the scope of this manual.[2] Here, we merely discuss survey issues likely to be of most concern to CDAs.

All CDAs, even small ones, can undertake customer surveys. While survey procedures can become quite sophisticated, for most CDA purposes, highly simplified survey procedures can be used and can provide reasonably accurate information.

Exhibits 7.5 and 6.6 provide examples of questionnaires that have been used to obtain evaluative feedback from clients on home improvement loans and housing counseling. Careful attention to the wording of questionnaires is important to ensure that clients understand what is being asked, that the questions only deal with topics clients have an ability to answer, and that the questions are not biased. (See chapter 6, Action 6.6(a) for more about client questionnaires.)

Combinations of telephone or in-person interviews and mailed questionnaires can be used. There are advantages and disadvantages to each method. CDAs will generally find it simplest and least expensive to survey customers by mail because, for most of their programs, customer names and addresses are readily available and mail surveys are generally inexpensive. However, their downside is

Exhibit 7.5

Example of Customer Survey Questionnaire

 CITY OF LONG BEACH DEPARTMENT OF COMMUNITY DEVELOPMENT

HOME IMPROVEMENT LOAN QUESTIONNAIRE

LONG BEACH
NEIGHBORHOOD
IMPROVEMENT
PROGRAM

1. HOW DID YOU HEAR ABOUT THE DEFERRED PAYMENT LOAN PROGRAM?

   A) NEWSPAPER. B) COMMUNITY MEETING/ORGANIZATION C) FRIEND/RELATIVE

   D) ANOTHER APPLICANT E) OTHER

   COMMENTS _____

   _____

   _____

2. THE SERVICE/INFORMATION YOU RECEIVED FROM THE CLERICAL STAFF WAS:

   A) EXCELLENT B) GOOD C) FAIR D) POOR

   COMMENTS _____

   _____

   _____

3. DID YOU HAVE ANY PROBLEMS SCHEDULING AN APPOINTMENT?

   A) YES B) NO

   COMMENTS _____

   _____

   _____

4. THE SERVICE/INFORMATION YOU RECEIVED FROM THE LOAN COUNSELOR WAS:

   A) EXCELLENT B) GOOD C) FAIR D) POOR

   COMMENTS _____

   _____

   _____

5. DID YOU FIND THE PROGRAM EASY TO UNDERSTAND?

   A) YES B) NO

   COMMENTS _____

   _____

   _____

6. THE SERVICE YOU RECEIVED FROM THE INSPECTOR WAS:

   A) EXCELLENT B) GOOD C) FAIR D) POOR

   COMMENTS _____

   _____

   _____

Exhibit 7.5 (continued)

7. THE SERVICE YOU RECEIVED FROM THE CONTRACTOR WAS:

   A) EXCELLENT   B) GOOD   C) FAIR   D) POOR

   NAME OF CONTRACTOR _____

   COMMENTS _____

   _____

   _____

8. WOULD YOU RECOMMEND THE CONTRACTOR TO A FRIEND?   A) YES   B) NO

   COMMENTS _____

   _____

   _____

9. WOULD YOU RECOMMEND THE DEFERRED LOAN PROGRAM TO A FRIEND?

   A) YES   B) NO

   COMMENTS _____

   _____

   _____

10. WHAT DID YOU LIKE MOST OVERALL ABOUT THE PROGRAM? _____

   _____

   _____ LEAST OVERALL? _____

   _____

   _____

11. DO YOU KNOW ABOUT OTHER PROGRAMS OFFERED THROUGH THE NEIGHBORHOOD PRESERVATION DIVISION?

   A) YES   B) NO

   IF NO, WOULD YOU LIKE INFORMATION MAILED TO YOU?   A) YES   B) NO

   PLEASE FEEL FREE TO USE THE SPACE BELOW TO COMMENT FURTHER ON ANY ASPECT OF THE PROGRAM OR GIVE SUGGESTIONS THAT MAY HELP US TO IMPROVE OUR SERVICE TO THE COMMUNITY.

   _____

   _____

   _____

   _____

   _____

   _____

   _____

Source: City of Long Beach, California, Department of Community Development, 1990.

that customers may not return completed questionnaires even when the latter are short and a self-addressed, stamped envelope is included. Nonetheless, mailed questionnaires may often be the most feasible approach, particularly when the agency wants feedback from a large number of clients, or if staff are not available to telephone or visit clients. When using mail surveys the CDA should provide subsequent mailings and/or telephone reminders to non-respondents in order to ensure adequate response levels.

In-person surveys are likely to be practical for a CDA only if the interviews are conducted as part of regular agency procedures, such as when an inspector visits a site for regular monitoring or evaluation purposes. In such cases, survey administration is quite inexpensive. However, if the agency wants to interview customers after they have received the service, in-person surveys can become expensive.

Telephone surveys are practical if the number of customers to be interviewed is small, staff time is available to make the calls, or money is available for contracting this work.

CDAs should seek response rates of 50 percent or more for surveys. To increase response rates to mail surveys, send second mailings to those clients who do not respond to the first. If the response rate is still below 50 percent, the agency can use a third mailing, make reminder telephone calls, or undertake phone interviews instead.

Surveys that involve many clients, such as the case with some service contracts, will probably need to be tabulated by computer, especially when the agency wants to get cross tabulations such as breakouts by section of the community, age group, race/ethnicity, and household size. Some effort will be required to enter the questionnaire data into the computer. Thus, client surveys involve time and effort and probably a small amount of out-of-pocket costs.

Except for large CDAs that survey large numbers of clients, CDAs are not likely to need to use a contractor to undertake customer surveys. However, the CDA should consider using a local survey expert to help with the initial design of the questionnaire and survey process to avoid biases and other problems.

Surveys of housing rehab clients do not appear to present any significant burden to CDAs, in part because staff inspect the work when completed and usually talk with the homeowner. A survey questionnaire can easily be administered at this point, as done in Rock Island (see chapter 6, Action 6.6(a)). Even a mail, telephone, or in-person survey administered 10 to 11 months later to identify the existence of problems before the warranty runs out does not seem likely to be an excessive burden for most CDAs.

Customers of CDA training or assistance programs (such as minority and small business owners or neighborhood organization personnel) can also be readily surveyed at the completion of training or assistance. Follow-up surveys are appropriate to assess the longer run impacts of such programs.

Cuyahoga County ➤ Cuyahoga County gives participants in its minority business development program a short questionnaire at the final session. A follow-up questionnaire is sent to participants about a year later asking whether they *have* started a business, what is preventing them from doing so, and if more training is needed.

Trained Observer Procedures

Observation of housing conditions, neighborhood cleanliness, condition of streets and sidewalks, and overall neighborhood appearance is an appropriate evaluation tool for some CDA programs. For example, observing housing conditions over a period of years gives an indication of the effects of CDA housing programs. Such information can also be used for planning purposes as discussed in chapter 8. These visual observations, sometimes called "windshield surveys," should be conducted by individuals who have received training in what to look for.

The following steps—based on practices Albany used to survey housing conditions in target areas—describe the procedures commonly followed for trained observer surveys:

1. Select the area to be surveyed.

2. Determine what data are to be collected, develop the survey instrument, and field test it. See exhibits 8.1 and 8.2 for examples of data collection instruments for visual inspections of business facilities and residential structures.

3. Train the observers to ensure that they use the same standards. For example, provide observers with examples of what a structure looks like in the different rating categories used in the survey (e.g., standard, some deterioration, heavy deterioration). Ideally, observers should visit structures in different conditions in the field. Otherwise, photos of structures in different conditions can be used to demonstrate the rating scales, as used in Kansas City. In Albany, planning staff trained four students from a nearby university to conduct an assessment of housing conditions.

4. Pilot test the survey. Check to see that the observers' ratings are reasonably accurate. Provide additional training if needed. Pilot testing also enables staff to determine how quickly observers can rate a specific area. This can be used to determine how many observers and how much time will be needed to conduct the survey.

5. Conduct the survey. In Albany, the field staff were organized in teams of two. This allows both sides of a street to be covered in one pass, is a more pleasant way to work, and provides back-up if one person runs into a problem. To prevent duplicate surveying of the same area by different observers, each observer should keep a record of the areas surveyed and report this on a daily basis. Albany staff used a city planning map to mark, on a daily basis, which streets had been surveyed. Charlotte contracted to a university for a large-scale survey of housing condition.

6. Conduct quality control checks to ensure data quality. The staff member responsible for quality control should go into the field to re-rate a sample of each observer's work (perhaps 10 percent). Daily checks are probably appropriate when observers are new. If the checks reveal very few, or no errors, fewer checks will be needed. In addition, ratings should be checked for completeness and accuracy in the office. One approach is to compare the results of observers in the same area. If observers work in teams of two, each rating one side of the street, generally their ratings should be similar. If they are quite different, this should be discussed with the observers to determine the reasons for the discrepancies.

7. Enter data as you proceed. Albany staff recommend that data entry proceed as the survey progresses. Data entry was done by observers, which provided a change of pace and was a good alternate activity during bad weather. Data entry also allows staff to see some of the results of their work.

An example from Kansas City, Missouri (see exhibit 7.6), provides a look at how the data obtained from the trained observer approach can be mapped, a graphic method that summarizes the findings in a readily understandable way. (For full details, see "Housing Conditions: Survey Results," Kansas City, Missouri, City Development Department, May 1989.)

Kansas City ➤ Kansas City has conducted periodic trained observer surveys of external housing conditions. Its most recent (1987/88) survey concentrated on the older neighborhoods of the city but included lower-income new areas. The trained observer uses a photographic rating scale procedure based on the "Texas Pictorial Method" (developed by the Texas Department of Community Affairs). Eight characteristics are rated using a 7-point rating scale: roof, exterior wall surfaces, porch and front entryways, doors, windows, lawn and shrubs, curbs and sidewalks on the property boundary, and neighborhood appearance. Each of the seven grades on the scale for each of the eight characteristics is associated with

EXHIBIT 7.6

Example of Displaying Results of Trained Observer Surveys

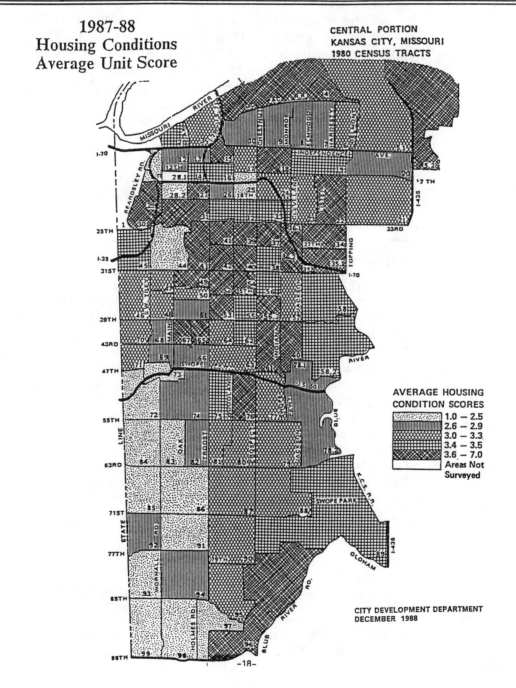

1987-88
Housing Conditions
Average Unit Score

CENTRAL PORTION
KANSAS CITY, MISSOURI
1980 CENSUS TRACTS

AVERAGE HOUSING
CONDITION SCORES
1.0 — 2.5
2.6 — 2.9
3.0 — 3.3
3.4 — 3.5
3.6 — 7.0
Areas Not
Surveyed

CITY DEVELOPMENT DEPARTMENT
DECEMBER 1988

Source: Kansas City, Missouri, City Development Department, "Housing Conditions Survey Results," May 1989.

photographs that visually describe the features of the particular grade.

Kansas City surveyed a sample of 20 percent of its housing units. Observers made assessments from the public right-of-way by comparing the structure to the photographs. The ratings for each characteristic were multiplied by a prescribed weight developed in past studies based on how well each characteristic reflected overall housing conditions. Scores from 1.0 to 2.9 were considered "sound"; 3.0 to 3.4 were considered appropriate for "minor rehab"; 3.5 to 4.4 signify the need for "major rehab"; and scores of 4.5 or greater are labelled "dilapidated."

For each census tract, the percentage of structures in each condition category and the average score were tallied, and changes in ratings from the previous survey were calculated.

Resources Required to Implement these Ideas

Resources needed for evaluation of CDA programs will vary by the size and complexity of the program(s) examined and the depth of the evaluation. Regular monitoring and documentation of results will facilitate performing periodic program evaluations.

Depending on the procedures used, volunteers or students can help keep down the costs of evaluation. Generally, however, to make the evaluation effective and reliable, someone trained in performing evaluations should oversee or advise the process.

Such procedures as customer surveys and trained observer procedures require time and effort, particularly at the beginning. Small CDAs will obviously need to use highly simplified versions of "big-city" procedures. However, they have the advantage of serving many fewer customers and having much smaller geographical areas for trained observers to cover.

Notes, chapter 7

1. Some sources of more detailed information on program evaluation procedures include: *Practical Program Evaluation for State and Local Government,* Second Edition (Washington, D.C.: The International City Management Association and The Urban Institute Press, 1981); *How Effective Are Your Community Services?* Second Edition (Washington, D.C.: The Urban Institute Press, 1991); and Sage Publications' "Program Evaluation Kit," Second Edition (Newbury Park, Calif.: Sage Publications, 1990).

2. Some sources of information on surveys include: *How to Conduct Surveys* (Beverly Hills, Calif.: Sage Publications, 1985); and *How to Conduct a Citizen Survey* (Chicago, Ill.: American Planning Association, 1987). Numerous more technical publications are available.

8

Long-Range (Strategic) Planning

ACTION 8.1 *Conduct Needs Assessments to Determine Future Needs*

8.1(a) Set the limits of the study, beginning with the identification of a CDA mission statement

8.1(b) Use a variety of procedures to obtain relevant needs information

8.1(c) Inventory existing programs and estimate their ability to meet future needs

8.1(d) Identify the major problems and obstacles to meeting future needs

ACTION 8.2 *Analyze Options and Strategies to Meet the Needs*

8.2(a) Develop the options to be analyzed

8.2(b) Examine the impacts, costs, timing, and feasibility of each option

ACTION 8.3 *Take Steps Throughout the Process to Encourage Use and Implementation of the Recommendations*

8.3(a) Involve major interest groups in the long-range planning activity

8.3(b) Include an action plan as part of the recommendations

8.3(c) Present the findings in a clear, attractive manner

8.3(d) Monitor the progress of implementation

8.3(e) Periodically update the needs assessment and analysis

Long-Range (Strategic) Planning

Community Development Agencies (CDAs) operate in a complex, changing environment. They are under pressure to deliver a wide range of activities to a diverse population. It is thus important that they periodically attempt to anticipate needs beyond the immediate year or two. This will enable them to be proactive rather than only reactive to current needs and to higher level government actions, such as federal and state legislation and regulations. In other words, CDAs should set aside the time to plan policies and programs that meet the changing needs of the people they are serving, and to recognize the restrictions they will likely face and need to overcome.

The term "strategic planning" is currently a hot term. Many people have difficulty distinguishing "strategic" from "long-range" planning. Some feel that strategic planning emphasizes implementation and that long-range planning does not. We use the term long-range planning (LRP) here, defining it as encompassing strategic planning, that is, including the development of an implementable plan of action.

LRP will be useful, and worth the effort, only to the extent that something positive is done with its findings. While those participating in an LRP effort may feel good about having been through the process even if nothing results, too many government LRP efforts have been undertaken with no results. We have found that this occurs because the effort was overly general, did not provide any feasible recommendations, did not contain anything resembling a plan of action, or was unable to get anyone's attention.

The three actions presented in this chapter are the major steps in the LRP process. The first two actions focus on technical issues. The third emphasizes the need to (a) translate the findings into an implementable action plan and (b) obtain input from key implementing groups throughout the process.

While it is beyond the scope of this report to delve into much technical detail, we will identify some key steps drawn from such CDAs as those of Fairfax County, Virginia; King County, Washington; Albany, New York; Rock Island, Illinois; and Lower Merion Township, Pennsylvania. The suggestions presented also draw from the literature on long-range/strategic planning.[1]

While some CDAs undertake periodic reviews of CDA programs, most efforts do not involve systematic examinations of the agency's mission, consideration of the future environment, nor an explicit identification and analysis of community development options. Thus, there does not appear to be a great deal of actual experience to draw on for comprehensive long-range planning.

ACTION 8.1

Conduct Needs Assessments to Determine Future Needs

(Primary Sources: Albany, New York; Charlotte, North Carolina; Fairfax County, Virginia; King County, Washington; Lower Merion Township, Pennsylvania; Roanoke, Virginia; Rock Island, Illinois)

Community development agencies inevitably lack resources to do everything they would like to do, or feel should be done, or that the citizens propose be done. CDAs need a way to decide which programs are needed, and for which client groups. The CDA needs to:

— Scope the needs assessment, including identification of a CDA mission statement;

— Collect necessary information on needs;

— Inventory relevant current programs and estimate the nature and magnitude of the likely future *unmet* needs; and

— Identify the major problems and obstacles to meeting future needs.

In this section, we briefly discuss each of these steps.

8.1(a)

Set the limits of the study, beginning with the identification of a CDA mission statement

An LRP effort can flounder and frustrate participants if it attempts to cover every possible external factor and every conceivable program and policy issue. Undertaking LRP for a CDA's whole mission would provide comprehensive coverage. We found only one such effort in our examination. A more realistic option, and one taken by a number of CDAs, is to focus on one of its major services at a time. The CDA, for example, might focus in alternate years on affordable housing, economic development for depressed areas of the community, a plan for the homeless, a plan for housing for other special populations, or social services needed by low-income families. This was done, for example, by Fairfax County (affordable housing), King County (the homeless and housing for special needs populations), Rock Island (housing), and Lower Merion Township (to maintain the vitality of a central business district).

If an agency does not already have a mission statement, as a first step it should develop one that includes objectives that are stated as specifically as possible. Even though some generality is unavoidable in such statements, they are crucial in putting some boundaries on the planning effort.

Rock Island ➤ The Rock Island Housing Task Force included this mission statement in its 1990 effort to develop a housing strategy: "To identify housing needs and opportunities, to recommend strategies to address the issues, and to suggest roles and responsibilities of various segments of the community in order to stabilize or improve neighborhood conditions, to promote new development and reinvestment, and to enhance Rock Island's image as a place to live."

Note that this mission statement identifies the mission for the strategy development team as well as for the whole community's housing program.

Long-range planning can also be done for individual neighborhoods. A preliminary needs assessment can be used to identify those neighborhoods particularly in need of major long-term assistance and, thus, for which a long-range strategic plan should be developed.

8.1(b) *Use a variety of procedures to obtain relevant needs information*

Typically, needs assessments seek the best, most accurate, data available on such elements as: the current level of need; the current services and programs available to meet the need (especially their capacity for the various categories of clients); the current unmet need; future trends in the number and types of clients; and information on current, and likely future, barriers and obstacles to providing the needed services.

Because of the complexity of community development needs, no single collection procedure is likely to be adequate for all these elements. Data collection procedures that CDAs can draw on include:

❑ Examination of existing public records from local, state, and federal agencies on housing, business conditions, and magnitude of recorded human service problems (such as unemployment, public assistance levels, housing vacancy rates, and housing program waiting lists).

❑ Surveys of physical conditions by trained observers (such as windshield surveys for assessing such conditions as: condition of housing and business facilities, vacant lots, street cleanliness, and other aspects of community appearance).

❑ Surveys of households, businesses, and "experts" concerning their needs and perceptions of problems in housing, business conditions, and needs for a variety of human services.

For example, to conduct an assessment of the need for affordable housing in the community, the CDA might seek estimates of the number of households of the following types, obtained from the sources indicated:

— Households living in sub-standard housing. Use windshield surveys (external conditions) and housing surveys (internal conditions)

— Households spending greater than 30 percent of their income on housing. Use household surveys.

— Households residing in assisted housing who are trying to make the transition to market-rate housing. Use household surveys and government records.

— Low- and moderate-income households who are seeking "starter homes." Use household surveys.

— Low- and moderate-income households who wish to enter the jurisdiction or move to other areas within the jurisdiction but are unable to find affordable housing. Use government records and household surveys.

The following sections discuss each of the three types of data collection procedures.

Examination of Public Agency Records

Data from a variety of local, state, and federal agencies are likely to be useful for most needs assessments.

For example, for housing needs assessments the CDA can obtain from government records data on:

— Number of owner-occupied and renter-occupied units;

— Number and percentage of vacancies;

— Waiting lists for housing and other assistance programs;

— Housing costs, both rental and owner-occupied, such as the median values;

— Financing charges; and

— Current rental rates for various categories of housing.

Most of the above data elements can be broken out by neighborhood and by size of house or household.

Federal and local census information will reveal the community's latest available demographic data such as population, household size, race/ethnicity, and income. Federal 1990 Bureau of the Census data, collected from all households, contains information by census tract on demographic and income characteristics of residents, type of building structure, number of rooms in the house or apartment, ownership of the house or apartment, estimated value of the property, and monthly rent. The 1990 Census also collected data from a sample (about one in six) of households on a variety of additional housing-related information such as utility costs, monthly mortgage payments, number of bedrooms, plumbing facilities, and building age. However, decennial federal Census data becomes outdated and decreases in value as the decade progresses. The CDA will need to tap the latest estimates of local and state planning agencies.

Information on publicly assisted individuals and households is usually available from state and local government social services departments, health agencies, employment agencies, and the housing agency.

Some data may be available only for the city or county as a whole and may not be available in sufficient detail, such as by neighborhood or by age or income group. Often, however, this problem can be alleviated by asking for special runs of the data by zip code or area code, if client addresses or telephone numbers are available.

Trained Observer Assessments of Physical Conditions

"Windshield" surveys can be used to assess the external or structural conditions of houses, buildings, lots, streets, and so on, especially for low-income areas. Many CDAs have used these surveys for a variety of purposes including input into needs assessments. Trained personnel using predesigned rating scales rate the condition of all or a sample of items within defined areas. This information can provide the CDA with a summary of facility conditions in various areas to help ensure that planning is based on an accurate assessment of current conditions. In addition to their use for LRP needs assessments, these procedures can also be used to evaluate the effectiveness of CDA programs, as well as to help the CDA develop annual action plans. Details on these procedures were presented in chapter 7, where these other uses are also discussed.

The data will be most useful if broken out by neighborhood, type of structure, whether residential or nonresidential, and whether the facility is vacant or occupied. For each group the number and percentage of structures in each condition can then be tabulated and presented. This is particularly important in developing strategies for individual neighborhoods.

For LRP purposes, it will normally be sufficient to assess a random sample of covered areas rather than all structures. The latter is more likely to be needed when trained observer procedures are used to help allocate the CDA's resources over the near future.

This type of procedure can also be used in obtaining needs data for specific programs. Both King County and Roanoke, for example, have used trained observers to count the number of people sleeping on the streets for planning emergency housing services. To reduce costs, the LRP team might use volunteers to make these counts (as done in Albany and Roanoke).

Exhibits 8.1 and 8.2 are examples of trained observer rating sheets that have been used to obtain needs assessment data on conditions of houses and their immediate surroundings, and the physical condition of a key business district serving less well-off areas of the community, respectively.

Below we detail some specific applications of the use of trained observers for needs assessments.

Albany ➤ Albany conducted windshield surveys to determine the housing condition of selected areas, using the data for both planning and budgeting. Albany collected data on the condition of the building (amount of deterioration), occupancy status, and type of building. Albany used interns to collect the data; it arranged with a Professor of Public Policy at the State University of New York to allow students to receive credit for participating in the windshield survey. Albany used four summer interns and one supervisor. The interns did the field survey work and performed most of the data entry. The supervisor was a full-time staff member who trained the interns, coordinated and supervised field work and data entry, and checked the data for accuracy. Data analysis was done by the supervisor. (Albany field tested the survey instrument in a few neighborhoods to determine the number of structures one person could survey per hour.)

EXHIBIT 8.1

Example of a Housing Survey Rating Sheet

Property Address Street _____

Street Name _____

I. Ground Condition: CC[1]   CC[1]

1. High grass, weeds, shrubs		3. Trash/garbage in alley, sidewalk	
2. Unsanitary, trash, garbage		4. Illegal use of lot	

II. Exterior Housing Conditions   CC[1]   CC[1]

A. Repair		B. Exterior Finish	
Exterior Siding		Paint	
Roofing		Main walls	
Gutters		Porch	
Windows		Steps	
Doors and Doorways		Doors	
Chimney		Exterior Buildings	
Porch		Garage	
Pavement		Storage Building	
Garage		Fence	
Foundation			

1. Condition Codes: Enter 1 to 5 rating based on the following definitions.
    1 = Minor maintenance problems involving mostly appearance and requiring little in the way of expenditures to correct.
    2 = Minor housing code violations and requiring minimum expenditures.
    3 = Serious maintenance problems, involving major structural, life-safety or health hazards.
    4 = Urgent safety or health related situation requiring "immediate" action (within 3 days).
    5 = Life-threatening situation.

Source: Extracted from the rating sheets used by the Cleveland, Ohio, Department of Community Development, 1990. The full Cleveland rating sheet calls for condition ratings for each side of the structure and for more details on property ownership.

EXHIBIT 8.2

Example of a Business Facility Survey Rating Sheet

Building Address:_____

Number of Stories: _____

Owner/Occupied: **Y   N**   Renter/Occupied **Y   N**

1st Floor Use: _____ Sq Footage:_____Parking Demand_____

2nd Floor Use: _____ Sq Footage:_____Parking Demand_____

3rd Floor Use: _____ Sq Footage:_____Parking Demand_____

Building Condition   Excellent _____ Good_____ Poor_____Comments:_____

General Appearance   Excellent _____ Good_____ Poor_____Comments:_____

Significant Architectural Features

Awning? Y   N
Other _____

Signs	Y	N
Window	__	__
Awning	__	__
Building	__	__
Free Standing	__	__
Temporary (in window)	__	__
Other	__	__

Property Maintenance   Excellent____Good____Poor____

Parking Spaces   Public (#) _____   Private (#) _____

Streetscape

   Furniture _____

   Sidewalks Y N   Condition: Excellent____Good____Poor____

   Curbs   Y N   Condition: Excellent____Good____Poor____

   Trees/shrubs _____

   Public Signs Y N _____

   Lighting   Y   N   _____

   Other _____

Source: Lower Merion Township, Pennsylvania, Office of Community Development, 1990.

Charlotte ➤ Charlotte contracted with the University of North Carolina at Charlotte to do its survey of housing and tabulate the data. The university tabulated the percentage of housing in each targeted census tract with "deteriorated and dilapidated structures" based on rating a sample of residences in each tract. It also estimated the number of city residences requiring "major" and "minor" repairs.

Lower Merion Township ➤ Lower Merion Township contracted with a private firm to conduct a needs assessment that examined a central business district in an area that was deteriorating and needed work to develop vitality. A major part of the needs assessment was a visual survey of individual businesses on each block. The data collection instrument used is shown in exhibit 8.2. The needs assessment also included a market analysis of the business district to determine the market potential for consumer spending. It used the results of an earlier consumer study that had been undertaken two years before. To obtain information on parking needs, the consultant collected data on all current parking facilities within the area and examined traffic circulation based on data from the township's police traffic unit, information on average daily counts from the Department of Transportation, and observation of pedestrian circulation within the area.

Surveys of Households, Businesses, and "Experts"

Surveys of households, businesses and experts can be used to obtain data on the needs of customers, problems they have in accessing CDA services, and any other obstacles to meeting their needs.

For *affordable housing* needs assessments, surveys of residents (such as undertaken by Fairfax County) can provide estimates of the number of families with low and moderate income that are, for example, spending excessive amounts on rent and mortgages; seeking to move from renting to owning; currently in need of assisted housing; living in overly crowded or otherwise sub-standard housing; and experiencing other major housing-related problems such as rodents and major landlord-tenant conflicts. Residents can be asked to identify any problems they have had in accessing the services of the CDA or other relevant agencies. Landlords and neighborhood associations can also be surveyed to obtain their perceptions of major problems.

For *business development* needs assessments, surveys of businesses in the community (such as undertaken by Rock Island) can identify major business concerns and suggestions for long-range improvements as well as indications of future plans such as expansions, cutbacks, moves, and reasons for them. Businesses can be asked to identify any problems in accessing public services.

For *human service* needs assessments, surveys of households can provide an estimate of the number of low- and moderate-income households in the community needing assistance such as financial counseling, transportation, employment and training, literacy improvement, and health services. Households can also be asked to identify any problems they have had in accessing public services.

The CDA can survey experts in the community, such as university specialists, key community leaders (from business, government, nonprofit organizations and interest groups), and service providers. These persons can be asked for their view of the long-range needs of the community. Service providers and various interest groups, for example, can be a good source of information about particular population groups—the homeless, elderly, youth, and other people with special needs such as the physically handicapped. Service providers can also be asked about the quantity of service they provide as well as their perceptions of the unmet needs and problems of their client population. In addition, service providers can be asked to administer questionnaires to their clients on behalf of the CDA, or to provide CDA staff access to their clients for this purpose.

These surveys require careful and professional administration to yield reliable, valid information. They generally involve additional time and costs. Survey procedures are discussed in chapter 7, Action 7.5. Here is one example of their application in needs assessments.

Fairfax County ➤ Fairfax County used a housing survey to obtain estimates of the number of households, by household size, with various (low) incomes. By subtracting the number of households that were being served by housing programs (obtained from agency records), the county estimated the potential additional need for affordable housing in the county based on the number of households spending too high a percentage of their monthly income on housing (greater than 30%). The survey was administered via mail to a sample of households in the county. The survey collected data on demographic characteristics of households (e.g. family size, age, sex, race/ethnicity, and income) and monthly rent or mortgage payments. Fairfax achieved a 60 percent response rate, mailing a postcard to each sampled household seven days after the mailing of the survey; the post card thanked those who had already responded to the survey and reminded those who had not. It later sent a special reminder to those households who had still not returned their completed questionnaires.

Rock Island ➤ Since 1986, Rock Island has annually interviewed a sample of its businesses. Each year the CDA interviews about 40 (mostly small) businesses. Owners or senior managers of the individual businesses are interviewed in-person by a senior CDA staff member about such issues as: the size of employment; the availability and quality of the local work-force; the local environment (such as labor attitudes, access to capital, energy costs, transportation services, insurance costs, and city, county, and state attitudes); various aspects of public services, including regulations, laws, and proce-dures; specific ways in which the CDA might assist their business including the information or assistance the busi-ness feels it wants or needs; and future plans for the business, including expansion and relocation intentions.

Such information provides considerable information useful for long-range planning for business opportunities in declining or dis-tressed areas. This procedure is described in more detail in chapter 2.

King County ➤ King County, in its assessment of emergency shelter needs, mailed a questionnaire to County shelter providers. It asked shelter managers to provide information about the capacity and specific services provided, the number and the type of clients (e.g., the sex, age group, household composition), financial information, the number of clients turned away, and the shelter manager's opinion about the homeless situ-ation in the County. (Two-thirds of the shelters completed questionnaires.) King County CDA also asked each provider to administer a questionnaire to a representative sample of clients. (The requested sample size was 100% for shelters with 30 or fewer beds, 50% with 31-100 beds, and 25% for shelters with over 100 beds.) The questionnaire was admin-istered by shelter staff to clients in the shelter on one night during the study period. The questionnaire asked about use of shelters, problems locating shelter space and emergency housing, and the kinds of non-shelter services the client needed. (For more information on this needs assessment, see "Homelessness Revisited: 1986 Seattle-King County Emergency Shelter Study Update," King County Depart-ment of Planning and Community Development, Septem-ber 1986.)

In addition to "systematic" surveys, a needs assessment team can use less formal survey techniques, ones that do not provide any statistical data. Such techniques can provide important insights into the major problems and obstacles that need to be overcome to provide services to low- and moderate-income households.

These techniques include such approaches as "focus groups." In such groups, 8 to 12 people such as community leaders, service providers, other experts, or clients, convene to discuss problems.

Discussions of approximately two hours are led by an experienced small-group facilitator, and are held in relaxed, pleasant settings.

Another less formal needs assessments technique is to seek input on needs, problems, and obstacles through public planning workshops and public hearings, as done in Roanoke (see Action 8.3(a)).

Finally, the CDA can use the media to obtain citizen input. This might be done by printing citizen surveys in the newspaper, or by using television or radio "call-in" formats.

Roanoke ➤ Roanoke used both newspaper and television to encourage citizen input for updating its comprehensive plan. A special insert was included in the Sunday newspaper on the day a television program on the planning process was broadcast. The insert included information about planning, community development issues, and a description of the process being used to update the comprehensive plan, and a questionnaire. The CDA and TV station jointly developed the half-hour television program. The program featured a series of interviews with city officials and citizens (as done in public affairs programs such as "Meet the Press"). Program panelists also urged citizens to complete and return the newspaper questionnaire. At the end of the program, a telephone number was announced for citizens to call in with any ideas or comments.

Example of Information Obtained from a Variety of Sources for a Needs Assessment

Exhibit 8.3 illustrates the findings that a needs assessment can provide, in this case on affordable housing needs, developed for the Fairfax County Affordable Housing Strategy effort.

The data collection procedures used included data from two different sources: the county's biennial survey of households and its housing program waiting list records.

8.1(c) *Inventory existing programs and estimate their ability to meet future needs*

A needs assessment should estimate not only the total future need but also the portion of it that is likely to be unmet. To accomplish this, the needs assessment team needs to examine not only the CDA's own current capacity, but that of programs of other relevant federal, state, and local government agencies, and the private sector. The surveys of service providers discussed under Action 8.1(b) can be used to request information on each provider's capacity.

EXHIBIT 8.3

Example of Findings from Needs Assessements

HOUSEHOLD SIZE	VERY LOW INCOME NUMBER OF HOUSEHOLDS	LOWER INCOME NUMBER OF HOUSEHOLDS	TOTAL HOUSEHOLDS
Unknown	–	–	425
1	7,366	4,111	11,477
2	3,213	2,363	5,576
3	5,380	1,366	6,746
4	1,961	3,096	5,057
5+	1,721	783	2,504
TOTAL	19,641	11,719	31,785

Number of Households Assisted   – 8,681
Total in Need   23,108

B. PERCENTAGE DISTRIBUTION OF AVERAGE DEMAND BY UNIT SIZE AND INCOME

Annual Income	Unit Size 1 BDRM	2 BDRM	3 BDRM	4 BDRM
$ 0 – 4,999	34%	21%	18%	16%
5,000 – 9,999	18	11	10	21
10,000 – 14,999	25	27	22	22
15,000 – 19,999	15	27	31	17
20,000 – 24,999	5	10	14	8
25,000 – 29,999	1	2	1	8
30,000 – 34,999	2	1	3	5
35,000+	0	1	1	3
	100%	100%	100%	100%

Source: "A Strategic Plan For Affordable Housing: Final Draft," Fairfax County Redevelopment and Housing Authority, Fairfax, Virginia, November 2, 1989.

Such surveys can also help distinguish how that capacity is allocated among types of potential clients. This can be done if capacity is broken out by such characteristics as: the type of client the provider is serving, e.g., only low-income households, the elderly, the homeless, the disabled, etc.; the location served by the provider, e.g., all neighborhoods or only some; and any other major eligibility requirements that may affect the use of the program for substantial numbers of the target population.

To estimate the current *unmet* need, the needs assessment team can then compare the available program capacity against the estimated total need (such as done in exhibit 8.3).

One key further step is to project the need in future years. The easiest, and most frequently applied, procedure is to assume that current need will continue into the indefinite future. However, the needs assessment team should consider trends that are likely to significantly add to or diminish needs. For example, a community may be facing an influx of new immigrants who will require added low-income housing, or may be facing the likelihood of the closing down or arrival of a major local employer. Although it is impossible to predict the future, estimates of future needs are the backbone of long-range planning and are necessary even if they are more rough than precise.

8.1(d) *Identify the major problems and obstacles to meeting future needs*

A major element of a long-range planning process is to identify the major problems and obstacles likely to hinder the CDA in meeting its estimated needs. The first obstacle, generally, is that of limited resources. Other obstacles may be government laws and regulations, possible opposition to needed programs and policies from interest groups, organizational issues, and physical limitations such as lack of available space for certain types of community improvements.

Information on major problems and obstacles can be obtained through the survey procedures discussed above. The needs assessment team can also obtain information from its own examination of existing legislation and regulations, as did the Fairfax County Affordable Housing and Rock Island Housing teams.

ACTION 8.2

> *Analyze Options and Strategies to Meet the Needs*
>
> (Primary sources: Fairfax County, Virginia; Rock Island, Illinois)

Once estimates of the type and magnitude of needs become available, the CDA needs to develop options and strategies to meet these needs. The long-range planning team then needs to determine which options/strategies are the most cost-effective, that is, have the highest likely impact considering likely resource availability. This step, based on our review, appears to be the one least systematically carried out by long-range planners.

8.2(a)   *Develop the options to be analyzed*

The information obtained during the needs assessment phase provides the starting point for developing the options. The choice of options to consider is critical since it will constrain the subsequent analysis and recommendations later brought to community decision makers.

Options should encompass not only current and new public programs but also changes to policies and to zoning and land use actions, to other laws and regulations, and possible efforts by the private sector including government financial and other incentives to encourage private assistance efforts.

Creative, innovative ideas are important here. Brainstorming can help bring in a wide range of viewpoints. The options need not be mutually exclusive. Final recommendations are likely to include a combination of actions.

Fairfax County   ➤ Fairfax County, in developing its affordable housing strategic plan, considered a wide range of alternatives for increasing housing production opportunities and reducing barriers to production. Options identified included: use of an affordable housing ordinance; changes in residential and mixed use development criteria; zoning changes; production of shared-housing units; production of various other types of dwelling units; and purchase of foreclosed houses.

Rock Island   ➤ Rock Island's Housing Task Force used a brainstorming approach to identify a range of options aimed at helping stabilize or improve neighborhood conditions. Some options it considered were: a mortgage credit certificate program; expanded use of various state housing financial assistance programs; a low-interest loan program for improving existing homes or purchasing vacant ones to be funded by a local foundation; expansion of financial incentives to encourage housing rehabilitation; expansion of programs to eliminate abandoned/boarded properties; more effective inspection of rental units; expansion of city legal support to help clean up problems (such as to speed up the demolition process); and more borrower education and counseling, especially for first time home buyers.

8.2(b)   *Examine the impacts, costs, timing, and feasibility of each option*

The point here is to analyze *each* major option, not, as seems to be more frequently done, quickly select a package and cost out only that recommended package. The availability of relatively inexpensive computer hardware and software means that CDAs now can more quickly analyze numerous options and combinations of options.

Impacts. The toughest and most neglected step in long-range planning is to provide estimates of the effects of each option on each objective identified at the beginning of the LRP process. To do this, the statement of objectives should be expressed in terms of specific measurable performance indicators. The LRP team might go further and develop an actual target for each indicator, phased over the next several years. This analysis might very well indicate that some of the targets are infeasible, making lower targets necessary.

Cost. The cost of each option should be estimated. For example:

Fairfax County ➤ In developing its strategic plan for affordable housing, Fairfax County estimated the cost of subsidies for each of five different income groups that the recommended option would help. It based these estimates on its estimates of the cost for providing affordable, reasonable-quality housing. The subsidy was calculated as the difference between the cost of providing a unit and the rent that each household could afford by spending 30 percent of its gross income on housing.

Timing. Different options are likely to yield results at different points in time; some will produce results quickly, others more slowly. The timing of the costs will also differ, especially relative to when their impacts occur. Thus, the costs and impacts of each option should be laid out over time. How far into the future do costs and impacts need to be estimated? This is difficult to determine. The basic principle is to estimate into the future no further than necessary to make choices. Five to ten years is a typical planning horizon.

Feasibility. Finally, each option should be assessed for legal, physical, financial, and political feasibility. Note, however, that in the long run, obstacles can often be overcome if time and effort are applied. At the very least, this step will later help the team lay out a feasible action plan for implementation of the recommended strategies. For example, the Fairfax County affordable housing strategy team felt that the costs of their initial housing production goal were to high, causing them to reduce their production goal.

Compare the options on cost, impacts, timing, and feasibility and develop recommendations.

Do not expect a clearcut winner. In most LRP efforts, the team will find that some options will be most favored for some objectives or criteria but not for others.

Exhibit 8.4 illustrates one type of quantitative output of a long-range planning effort. It indicates the number of housing units in each income category that would be assisted in future years by the recommended option proposed by the Fairfax County LRP team. The exhibit also presents the estimated costs for serving each income category.

Fairfax County ➤ The Fairfax County experience illustrates the need to analyze the diverse tradeoffs that planners and policymakers need to consider in LRPs. The Fairfax County Planners found that assistance costs varied greatly among types of households needing housing assistance. Families living in poverty required deep subsidies. Families of low and moderate wage earners required only moderate and perhaps only temporary subsidies. And some families needed only modest assistance to gain entry into an affordable housing situation (e.g., home ownership). If only households at the very lowest income levels were considered, the number of units that could be subsidized (through rental payments or construction) would be highly limited because of the high expense of each unit. Alternatively, if households at the other end of the spectrum were targeted, a greater number of households could be helped, but they would not be those in the greatest need. The planners estimated the costs and housing units gained for each of a number of combinations between the extremes of maximizing unit production and serving lowest income households. Exhibit 8.4 presents the costs and housing impacts if one such option, their recommended option, is implemented.

ACTION 8.3

Take Steps Throughout the Process to Encourage Use and Implementation of the Planning Recommendations

(Primary sources: Fairfax County, Virginia; Lower Merion Township, Pennsylvania; Roanoke, Virginia; Rock Island, Illinois)

Even the best technical analysis can flounder and remain unused unless the LRP process takes steps to increase the likelihood that there will be a receptive audience. This section offers suggestions on these steps.

EXHIBIT 8.4

Example of Quantitative Output of a Long-Range Planning Effort for Affordable Housing

SUBSIDY COSTS BY INCOME LEVELS
USING RENT OR CAPITAL SUBSIDY FORMS
TO ACHIEVE FCRHA RENTAL PRODUCTION GOAL

ANNUAL INCOME RANGE	PERCENTAGE DISTRIBUTION	NUMBER OF UNITS	RENT SUBSIDY FORM ANNUAL UNIT RENT SUBSIDY	TOTAL ANNUAL RENT SUBSIDY	OR	CAPITAL SUBSIDY FORM ONE-TIME CAPITAL SUBSIDY	+	OPERATING SUBSIDY
$ 0	7%	225	$11,592	$2,608,200	OR	$17,964,800	+	$711,182
1,000	0%	0	11,292	0		0		0
2,000	1%	32	10,992	351,744		2,566,400		82,349
3,000	9%	289	10,692	3,089,988		23,097,600		654,528
4,000	5%	161	10,392	1,673,112		12,832,000		316,507
5,000	6%	193	10,092	1,947,756		15,398,400		320,864
6,000	3%	96	9,792	940,032		7,699,200		131,560
7,000	4%	128	9,492	1,214,976		10,265,600		136,917
8,000	3%	96	9,192	882,432		7,699,200		73,816
9,000	3%	96	8,892	853,632		7,699,200		44,944
10,000	4%	128	8,592	1,099,776		10,265,600		21,429
11,000	3%	96	8,292	796,032		7,699,200		0
12,000	5%	161	7,992	1,286,712		12,607,292		0
13,000	4%	128	7,692	984,576		9,707,236		0
14,000	5%	161	7,392	1,190,112		11,660,798		0
15,000	6%	193	7,092	1,368,756		13,425,062		0
16,000	5%	161	6,792	1,093,512		10,714,305		0
17,000	4%	128	6,492	830,976		8,192,847		0
18,000	4%	128	6,192	792,576		7,814,249		0
19,000	3%	96	5,892	565,632		5,576,739		0
20,000	3%	96	5,592	536,832		5,292,791		0
21,000	1%	32	5,292	169,344		1,669,614		0
22,000	1%	32	4,992	159,744		1,574,965		0
23,000	1%	32	4,692	150,144		1,480,316		0
24,000	1%	32	4,392	140,544		1,385,666		0
25,000	1%	32	4,092	130,744		1,291,017		0
26,000	1%	32	3,792	121,344		1,196,368		0
27,000	1%	32	3,492	111,744		1,101,718		0
28,000	1%	32	3,192	102,144		1,007,069		0
29,000	1%	32	2,892	92,544		912,420		0
30,000	1%	32	2,592	83,944		817,770		0
31,000	1%	32	2,292	73,344		723,121		0
32,000	1%	32	1,992	63,744		628,472		0
33,000	1%	32	1,692	54,144		533,822		0
34,000	0%	0	1,392	0		0		0
35,000	0%	0	1,092	0		0		0
TOTAL		3208		$25,560,036 PER YEAR	OR	$222,500,857 ONE TIME	+	$2,493,097 PER YEAR

Source: Fairfax County, Virginia, "Final Draft: A Strategic Plan for Affordable Housing," Fairfax County Redevelopment and Housing Authority, November 2, 1989.

8.3(a): *Involve major interest groups in the long-range planning activity*

From the beginning CDAs should involve representatives of major community interest groups in the long-range planning effort. A planning process undertaken solely by CDA staff would be much quicker, but participation by representatives of other concerned parties is likely to introduce more reality into the plan, enable the plan to get more community support, and greatly ease the task of implementation. Below is advice on how such involvement can be encouraged.

— Form an LRP advisory committee that includes representatives from community organizations, business, and special interest groups. This is commonly done by CDAs.

— Throughout the planning effort, review key elements of the analysis with the ultimate decision-making body (bodies). Discuss with them such elements as the scope of the LRP effort, key assumptions to be used in the analysis, the options to consider, and what elements ("variables") the planners expect to consider in the analysis.

Fairfax County ➤ Fairfax County staff found that once they began discussing their affordable housing strategy analysis with members of the County's Redevelopment and Housing Authority, one of the major customers for the strategy, those members not only helped improve the strategy but also became much more supportive of it and the ultimate recommendations.

— Hold public planning workshops to obtain input from the general public. These should make the final product more acceptable to community interest groups and give the final report more public credibility.

Roanoke ➤ Roanoke held a series of such workshops (held approximately one month apart) to identify community concerns, issues and options. At each meeting, small groups addressed one of three topics: neighborhood preservation and development, economic development, and city services and facilities. The last meeting was used to obtain feedback on a staff draft of a plan based on issues raised in the prior meetings.

➤ Roanoke's *neighborhood* planning process worked in a similar fashion. The city held three workshop meetings (also one month apart) in each neighborhood. At the first meeting participants identified and prioritized (by voting) neighborhood issues and concerns. At the second meeting, with assistance from staff of various city departments, the groups discussed potential solutions to deal with these issues. At the final meeting, CDA planning staff presented a draft neighborhood plan. The plan included "action strategies" identifying specific actions for resolving each issue and who would be involved in taking the actions (such as various city departments, the neighborhood organization, city council, etc.). Citizens discussed the draft plan and provided suggestions for improving it.

— Hold public hearings. While the persons attending may not be representative of the community, they can provide ideas as to the pulse of the community. One way to increase representativeness is to invite leaders or members of various sectors of the community.

— Obtain staff input on major program problems, ways to alleviate them, and strategy options. By staff, we mean here not just CDA personnel staffing the LRP process, but personnel throughout the agency. CDA employees are a major interest group and should be highly knowledgeable about the community's situation.

8.3(b)   *Include an action plan as part of the recommendations*

Action plans help set the stage for and encourage implementation of recommended strategies. Action plans should indicate who (both inside and outside the CDA) is to do what, by when, at what cost, and with what estimated results. The action plans need not be very detailed until the strategy has been officially approved.

Rock Island   ➤ Rock Island's Housing Task Force report identified actions needed for each of its strategies, focusing primarily on actions needed over the next 1-2 years. These actions identified which organization (city or an outside organization) needed to take the action.

Lower Merion Township   ➤ Lower Merion Township's study of a distressed business district included a time-phased plan that identified for each of the next five years the major needed actions, each action's estimated cost, and the funding sources for each.

Action plans provide a basis for continuing effort and for tracking progress. They can make the difference between a plan gathering dust and one that moves the community.

8.3(c)   *Present the findings in a clear, attractive manner*

This applies to all reports that a CDA prepares for outside use. Because quantitative personnel sometimes assume too much reader knowledge of their jargon and technical methods, the LRP team needs to be particularly careful to provide clear, understandable summaries and to fully explain the findings.

A summary of the findings and recommendations will also need to be presented *orally,* probably many times. The LRP team should rehearse their presentations and use attractive, clear visual aids, especially for the numerical findings.

8.3(d)   *Monitor the progress of implementation*

Once a strategy has been approved, the CDA should track progress and bring gaps and problems to the attention of those who approved the plan. Such tracking can be used to alert the organization that changes need to be made in the implementation strategy. These may include reallocating resources or reassigning staff or organizations to carry out the strategy. The agency may need to reconvene the original task force or committee if the situation warrants.

Fairfax County   ➢   Fairfax County is conducting annual evaluations of its Strategic Plan for Affordable Housing. The findings will be presented to the County Board of Supervisors. The evaluations will focus on progress on funding the planned steps, in making regulatory changes (i.e., land use policies, zoning, etc.), and housing unit production activity as compared to targets.

8.3 (e)   *Periodically update the needs assessment and analysis*

Ideally, a CDA is always acting under a long-range, strategic plan. A chronic problem with long-range planning is that as time goes on, circumstances change, often substantially. While the long-range planning process should attempt to anticipate changes, unforeseen circumstances will inevitably make some of the original strategy obsolete. At the very least, new circumstances will require adjustments.

The CDA will probably not need to completely redo the LRP process every year, but it should update the data on supply and demand and the time schedule. This information will indicate to the CDA what mid-course corrections are needed. Plan review and updating should probably be done every other year.

Fairfax County ➣ Fairfax County expects to update its data on housing needs and supply for its Affordable Housing Strategy every two years as new data on county population and housing becomes available.

Resources Required to Implement these Ideas

Both large and small CDAs can apply the ideas in this chapter. Smaller CDAs will generally have less resources to commit to a long-range planning effort and less ability to tap outside organizations for help. But because these CDAs require a less complex planning effort, they will need fewer resources for the LRP process than large CDAs.

Smaller communities also have the advantage that information may be more readily available, pockets of poverty and need are easier to identify, and employment information is easier to quantify because of the smaller number of businesses. This means that the planning analysis can be much simpler than in larger communities where more complex elements are likely to exist.

Size should not be an excuse for a CDA not to undertake a long-range, strategic, planning effort at least once every few years for its major functions.

Note, chapter 8

1. See, for example, "A Strategic Planning Guide," Public Technology, Inc., Washington, D.C., 1984; "Needs Assessment: A Workbook for Seattle Neighborhoods," Seattle Office of Neighborhoods, Seattle, Wash., September 1989; and United Way of America's "COMPASS" Report Series, Alexandria, Va., 1987. The latter contains individual reports describing household surveys, key informant surveys, service provider surveys, and the collection of social and economic data. While the focus of this series is on human services, most of the procedures are also applicable to housing and community development needs.

9

Putting These Ideas to Work

The previous chapters have identified more than 125 actions that encourage excellence in managing community development agencies. How do suggestions in these chapters relate to one another? How might a CDA use these ideas to encourage excellence?

Interrelationship of Themes and Actions

The actions in the previous chapters describe a collection of organizational and individual behaviors and characteristics that promote excellence. The chapter themes contribute to an organizational culture that puts a premium on participation, service to the client, and an on-going, continuous quest for improvement.

These themes interrelate and support one another, and sometimes overlap and interact with each other. For example:

— Encouraging employee involvement sets the stage for employee outreach to customers. Only motivated employees will put themselves out for the client and help bring about closeness to the customer.

— Making more efficient use of resources by streamlining and decentralizing decisions is based on the premise that people need some flexibility as to how they do their work. Keeping the number of required approvals to a minimum not only provides quicker response, it also indicates that management has faith in the employees, encourages responsibility and initiative, and reinforces the belief that the organization values its people.

— Contracting for performance not only encourages contractors to focus on and improve the quality of service, but is a major way to improve the productivity of the organization.

— While long-range planning at first glance may seem to be a separate element, it is not. The process of periodically examining the organization mission, its long-term objectives, and strategies to achieve those objectives, serves as a major building block to encourage a focus on customers in a way that should stimulate all employees to work toward those objectives. Providing opportunities for input from citizens and agency employees will help ensure that the objectives focus on the results desired.

— A number of procedures, particularly the use of trained observers and customer surveys, facilitate implementation of several themes. For example, both of these data collection procedures are suggested for CDA use in: developing information about community needs for long-range planning, periodically monitoring and evaluating the performance of contractors for improved performance, and periodically evaluating agency programs to identify problems that exist and constructive action that is needed.

When deciding which actions to implement, CDA managers should be aware that these themes are interrelated and many actions contribute to more than one purpose. Progress in any one theme is likely to also affect progress in others as well.

Some Suggestions for Implementing these Ideas

Each agency starts with its own organization, its own people, its own environment, and its own constraints. Any manager needs to consider these actions in the context of the CDA's current culture and needs.

First, we suggest that agency managers take an inventory of their own situation to determine where their strengths and weaknesses lie.

For example, does the manager feel that the agency needs to improve its closeness to customers? Can it use more involvement of its employees to improve service quality? Is it effectively contracting for performance rather than merely contracting to get work done?

Managers should not feel that they are dealing alone with the task of achieving excellence. Soliciting ideas from employees, forming ad hoc task groups, and encouraging discussion at staff meetings to discuss themes presented in this report are some practical ways of getting started.

One city that reviewed a draft of this manual divided the chapters among staff and asked them to pick out ideas and practices that could be implemented in their units. This effort started the ball rolling and resulted in several ideas being implemented.

Some of the ideas presented here require substantial effort to implement, others are simple and direct. None of these actions are intended to be blockbusters. Rather, the principle behind this manual is that little things mean a lot, particularly when lots of these little things are used, and are used continuously.

Some of the ideas presented in these chapters require larger scale efforts:

— Problem solving work-groups or teams, used by Santa Ana, San Mateo County, and Pinellas County.

— Roanoke's extensive efforts to have each neighborhood participate in a series of neighborhood workshops, as well as a set of city-wide workshops, to provide input into community planning.

— Norman's system of neighborhood-based and city-wide meetings and an advisory committee to provide input for community development project selection.

— Charlotte's extensive performance measurement process that collects productivity and service quality data on key objectives for each work unit.

— Knoxville's annual action plan development process, which includes the use of a two-day all-staff retreat and separate divisional meetings before and after, to seek comment from all staff.

— Fairfax County's extensive, long-range strategic planning effort for affordable housing.

— Rock Island annual business connection survey process, in which CDA staff along with business volunteers interview a sample of business officials to identify ways service can be improved and to obtain information for planning.

In contrast to these large efforts are numerous smaller initiatives such as the following:

— Rock Island's contacting each housing rehab client by phone a few weeks before the end of the warranty period to remind clients to check the work covered by the warranty.

— Albany's and Long Beach's outreach efforts to promote use of CDA programs by minorities and underserved customers.

— Roanoke's neighborhood liaisons sitting in on meetings their clients have with other agencies to help prevent antagonism and to help clients work within the system.

— Seattle's involving local businesses in developing written promotional materials to market neighborhood business districts to newcomers.

— Cleveland's regular meetings with its contractors to identify and address their concerns.

— Training workshops for minority business in Cuyahoga County, Cleveland, and Albany.

— The emphasis on teamwork in Lower Merion Township, Santa Ana, San Mateo County, and King County.

— Knoxville's willingness on the part of top management to meet everyday with staff, have regular all-staff monthly meetings, and other special activities that reach out to employees.

One crucial point: the *way* a manager goes about implementing and encouraging excellence is as important as the action itself. Staff and customer participation are essential to excellence; if either group is excluded from the process, the actions will not be successful.

Finally, it seems clear that excellence is an eternal quest. As soon as one improvement is made, another opportunity presents itself. Part of the vitality of the community development agency is the realization that the job is never done.

APPENDIX A

18 Primary Sites from which Examples have been Drawn

Agency Site	Director	Main Contact	Address
Albany, NY	Joseph Pennisi	Thomas Griner, Deputy Commissioner	Department of Housing and Community Development 155 Washington Ave. Albany, NY 12210 518/434-5240
Charlotte, NC	J.W. Walton	Patty Davis, Supervisor, Program Analysis, Budget and Planning	Community Development Department 600 East Fourth St. Charlotte, NC 28202 704/336-2016
Cleveland, OH	Chris Warren	Diane Corcelli, Manager of Public Information	Department of Community Development 601 Lakeside Ave. Cleveland, OH 44114 216/664-4011
Cuyahoga County, OH	Nancy Cronin	Katherine McHale, Manager, Community Development Div.	Department of Development 112 Hamilton Ave. Cleveland, OH 44114 216/443-7260
Fairfax County, VA	Walter Webdale	Audrey Spencer Horsley, Chief Planner, Community Development Div.	Department of Housing and Community Development One University Plaza Fairfax, VA 22030 703/246-8300

Agency Site	Director	Main Contact	Address
Hartford, CT*	Linda Bayer	Linda Bayer	Office of Community Development and Planning 942 Main Street Hartford, CT 06103 203/722-6490
Kansas City, MO*	James Vaughn	John Tangeman, Director of Planning and Development	Department of Housing and Community Development 14th Floor, City Hall 414 E. 12th Street Kansas City, MO 64106 816/274-2201
King County, WA	Miriam Greenbaum	Linda Peterson, Acting Chief, Community Development Section	Planning and Community Development Division 707 Smith Tower Bldg. 506 Second Ave. Seattle, WA 98104 206/296-8643
Knoxville, TN	J. Laurens Tullock	Wayne Blasius, Deputy Director	Department of Community Development 400 Main Ave. Knoxville, TN 37901 615/521-2120
Long Beach, CA	Susan Shick	Lawrence Triesch, Administrative Officer	Department of Community Development 333 West Ocean Blvd. Long Beach, CA 90802 213/590-6841
Lower Merion Township, PA	Ann Hutchin	Ruth Friedman, Community Development Administrator	Department of Planning and Community Development 75 E. Lancaster Ave. Lower Merion Township, PA 19003 215/645-6118
Norman, OK	**	Linda Price, Community Development Coordinator	Planning Department 201 West Gray P.O. Box 370 Norman, OK 73070 405/366-5439

Agency Site	Director	Main Contact	Address
Pinellas County, FL	Darlene Kalada	Darlene Kalada	Community Development Department 14 S. Ft. Harrison Ave. Suite 3050 Clearwater, FL 34616 813/462-4851
Roanoke, VA	**	Marie Pontius, Grants Monitoring Administrator	Office of Grants Compliance Municipal Bldg., RM 362 215 Church Ave., S.W. Roanoke, VA 24011 703/981-2344
Rock Island, IL	Gregory Champagne	Gregory Champagne	Community and Economic Development Department 1528 Third Ave. Rock Island, IL 61201 309/793-3350
San Mateo County, CA	Susan Wilson	Susan Wilson	Housing and Community Development Division 805 Veteran's Bldg., Suite 322 Redwood City, CA 94063 415/363-4451
Santa Ana, CA	Cynthia Nelson	Patricia Whitaker, Housing Manager	Community Development Agency 20 Civic Center Plaza Santa Ana, CA 92701 714/667-2200
Seattle, WA	David Moseley	Dick Woo, Block Grant Administrator	Department of Community Development 700 Third Ave., 8th Floor Seattle, WA 98104 206/684-0319

* No site visit was conducted at these sites; information was obtained through written materials and telephone interviews.

**There is no community development agency at these sites.

Characteristics of Sites from which Examples Have Been Drawn

Location	Agency Name	Population	Number of CDA Personnel
Albany, NY	Department of Housing and Community Development	97,000	31
Charlotte, NC	Community Development Department	383,000	58
Cleveland, OH	Department of Community Development	536,000	330
Cuyahoga County, OH	Community Development Division	650,000	21
Fairfax County, VA	Department of Housing and Community Development	770,853	208
Hartford, CT	Office of Community Development and Planning	137,980	15
Kansas City, MO	Department of Housing and Community Development	425,000	37
King County, WA	Planning and Community Development Division	1,362,000	8
Knoxville, TN	Department of Community Development	173,210	34
Long Beach, CA	Department of Community Development	400,000	107
Lower Merion Township, PA	Department of Planning and Community Development	59,737	4
Norman, OK	Planning Department[*]	80,000	4
Pinellas County, FL	Community Development Department	815,000	19
Roanoke, VA	Office of Grants Compliance[*]	100,100	2
Rock Island, IL	Community and Economic Development Department	43,700	19
San Mateo County, CA	Housing and Community Development Division	613,000	16
Santa Ana, CA	Community Development Agency	236,780	92
Seattle, WA	Department of Community Development	486,200	110

* There is no community development agency at these sites.

APPENDIX B:
Illustrative Performance Indicators for Community Development Agency Programs

Notes

1. This table presents illustrative indicators of service outcome/quality and productivity/efficiency — indicators currently not in wide use. Indicators of workload and workload accomplished are widespread among CDAs and are not repeated here.

2. This appendix is intended to help CDAs: (a) evaluate their programs periodically, (b) monitor and evaluate the performance of their contractors and (c) assess productivity improvement efforts. These three purposes are discussed in chapters 6 and 7.

3. The letters in the "Data Source" column refer to the following data sources:

    > A = Agency records;
    > B = Ratings by trained observers;
    > C = Surveys of customers;
    > D = Special analyses of business reports.

I. Housing Development and Human Services Programs

| | Data |
| Performance Indicators | Source |

A. *Housing Rehabilitation*

Outcome/Quality Indicators

1. Number of rehabs completed satisfactorily.	A, B, and C
2. Percentage of eligible units rehab passing inspection.	A
3. Average time between: (a) acceptance of rehab application and start of rehab work; (b) start and finish of rehab work; and (c) overall time between acceptance of application and *satisfactory* completion.	A
4. Percentage of units for each of (a), (b), and (c) in #3 completed within pre-set target durations.	A
5. Number and percentage of total units requiring corrections during rehab or after "complete," e.g., under terms of warranty.	A
6. Percentage of rehab jobs for which the customers rated the service provided by both the contractor and CDA as fully satisfactory.	C
7. Size of backlog waiting for rehab.	A
8. Percentage of customers who rated as satisfactory the time required for completion of rehabs.	C
9. Percentage of (a) CDA inspectors and (b) customers who rated the quality of the rehab work as "good".	B and C
10. Percentage of participating households rating the service/information provided by the agency staff as excellent or good.	C
11. Percentage of participating households rating the service received from the inspectors as good or excellent.	C
12. Percentage of *unsuccessful* applicants who rated as satisfactory: (a) the time required to get their answer, (b) the conduct of CDA staff during this experience with the agency, and (c) the fairness of the decision.	C

Efficiency Indicators

1. Staff work hours per unit rehabilitated or number of units rehabilitated per staff hour.   A

2. Cost per unit rehabilitated to at least *adequate* quality, broken out by (a) CDA administrative costs and (b) contract costs.   A, B, and C

3. Cost per unit rehabilitated that both the customer and CDA inspector rated as being of "good" (not just adequate) quality.   A, B, and C

B. Assistance in Such Human Service Activities as Counseling, Training, Transportation Services, and Child Care Services

Outcome/Quality Indicators

1. Total number of customers (individuals/families/households) assisted.   A

2. Percent of customers assisted within "X" weeks of request for help.   A

3. Number and percentage of customers who completed training satisfactorily or who completed the activity for which they were trained (e.g., weatherization).   A or B

4. Percentage of participants rating the assistance provided as having significantly reduced the problem for which assistance was sought.   C

5. Percentage of participants who rated as satisfactory, (a) the time required for applications to be processed, and (b) the overall time from the request until the service was actually delivered.   C

Productivity/Efficiency Indicators

1. Number of staff hours per customer assisted.   A

2. Cost per customer assisted who also rated the assistance as having significantly reduced the problem for which assistance was sought.   A and C

C. Help for the Homeless

Outcome/Quality Indicators

1. Total number of beds of acceptable quality made available.   A

2. Average number of persons per day (a) housed and (b) fed at least one meal per day.   A

3. Estimated percentage of need for beds filled on the average.   A and B

4. Estimated percentage of needed meals filled on the average.   A and B

5. Percentage of participants who rated as acceptable (a) the shelter provided and (b) the meals.   C

Productivity/Efficiency Indicators

1. Cost per bed-day used by homeless persons.   A

2. Cost per meal provided to homeless persons.   A

D. Code Enforcement

Outcome/Quality Indicators

1. Number of complaints received relating to need for code enforcement.   A

2. Percentage of inspections conducted within "X" days of a complaint.   A

3. Percentage of inspections showing sub-standard conditions.   A and B

4. Number and percentage of code enforcement violations brought into compliance.   A and B

5. Number and percentage of code enforcement violations brought into compliance within "Y" days from when a complaint was received or when code enforcement staff identified a violation.   A and B

6. Percentage of persons who complained about a violation (e.g., renters) who rated the CDA's violation-handling process as "good" or "excellent."   C

7. The percentage of persons against whom violations were brought by the CDA who reported that the CDA's handling of the process was fair.   C

Productivity/Efficiency Indicators

1. Number of staff hours per inspection.   A

2. Number of staff hours per code enforcement violation.   A

3. Number of staff hours per code enforcement violation that was corrected.   A and B

4. Cost per inspection.   A

5. Cost per violation processed.   A

6. Cost per violation that was corrected.   A and B

II. Economic Development Programs

Performance Indicators	Data Source

A. *Financial Assistance to Businesses*

Outcome/Quality Indicators

1.	Number of permanent jobs created/retained by participating business, both (a) total and (b) low-income, minority.	A, C, and D
2.	Additional tax revenues generated.	A, C, and D
3.	Average time from receipt of application until decision.	A
4.	Percentage of applications decided upon within "X" weeks of receipt.	A
5.	Percentage of participants rating the service of the program as "excellent" or "good."	C
6.	Percentage of *unsuccessful* applicants rating as satisfactory:(a) the time required to get their answer, (b) the conduct of the CDA staff during this experience with the agency, and (c) the fairness of the decision.	C

Productivity/Efficiency Indicators

1.	Cost per job created/retained.	A, C, and D
2.	Number of work hours per job created/retained.	A, C, and D

B. *Technical Assistance to Businesses*

Outcome/Quality Indicators

1.	Percentage of assisted businesses rating the service/information provided by the agency "excellent" or "good."	C
2.	Number and percentage of businesses assisted that rate the assistance as having made a positive contribution to their business.	A and C
3.	Number and percentage of businesses that reported that the assistance had made a significant contribution to their being able to create or retain jobs.	A and C

4. Number of jobs created/retained estimated to have resulted in part because of the assistance.   C

5. Percentage of businesses that rated as satisfactory the duration of time from the request for assistance until it was provided.   C

Productivity/Efficiency Indicators

1. Total number of assistance staff hours divided by the number of businesses that reported that the assistance had made a positive contribution to their business.   A and C

2. Total number of assistance staff hours divided by the number of jobs estimated to have been created or retained at least in part because of the assistance.   A and C

C. Enhancement of Targeted Commercial Areas

Outcome/Quality Indicators

1. Number and percentage of businesses reporting an improvement in sales due to improvements made by this program.   C

2. Net number of stores opening since the completion of the enhancements (netting out departures).   B

3. Percentage increase in pedestrian/traffic counts in commercial areas since completion of enhancements.   B

4. Number and percentage of businesses reporting that the help provided by the CDA made a significant improvement to (a) their own business and (b) business in general in the targeted area.   C

5. Percentage of businesses that applied for assistance that rated as satisfactory (a) the time required to obtain assistance and (b) the helpfulness of the CDA staff.   C

6. Number of jobs created or retained estimated to have resulted at least in part from the assistance.   A, B, and C

Productivity/Efficiency Indicators

1. Cost per business assisted.   A

2. Number of jobs created or retained per program dollar.   A, B, and C